M...
A MEN...OR?

A CALL TO ACTION IN A
DISCONNECTED WORLD

Serve the Lord with gladness!

Ken Black

Ken Black

outskirts
press

Me a Mentor? is dedicated to:

Carol Gienapp, my cousin, who fully supported my dream to serve in the mentoring field. She provided the inspiration, encouragement, and the vision to make it happen.

In Memory of Carol Gienapp

1944-2018

Rev. Charles Mueller Sr., my mentor, who was always there for me with encouraging words, dependable advice, and a loving spirit.

TABLE OF CONTENTS

FOREWORD
WHAT IS A MENTOR?

By Rev. Charles Mueller Sr.

Mentor. Even without fully knowing what it means, the word itself suggests mystery and adventure. Maybe that's because it is not just one word but three. It can be someone's name, it may be a verb, and it could be a noun.

For the longest time, stretching back to ancient history with a bit of Greek mythology mixed in, *Mentor* was the name of a trusted friend and advisor to King Odysseus. When Odysseus left to fight the Trojan wars, Mentor was one of those put in charge of the kingdom with an added duty of caring for Telemachus, the king's young son. And so it was that for centuries, Mentor was remembered and celebrated as a coach, as a friend, and as the faithful advisor to Odysseus' son. When spelled with a capital "M," the word Mentor is the name of a man who lived long ago and who helped guide a young man as he matured. But there is more.

Years passed until in 1699, *mentor* appeared in a French

publication in which it was spelled with a lowercase "m" and was used as a verb. It was used to describe a process over time by which an older person gave guidance and encouragement to one who was younger. It is not clear what kind of *mentoring* was provided, but it was given by someone who seemed more like a friend rather than a professional teacher or a trained tutor.

From *mentoring*, it's not much of a leap to a third use in which *mentor* is a noun describing a person (or people) who is on the scene offering a listening ear, an affirming attitude, and sometimes a helping hand. Over time, the younger seeker has come to be known as a *mentee*. The mentor/mentee relationship is an easygoing, casual relationship primarily concerned with the needs of the mentee. The pleasure a mentor can also derive from this relationship is an enormously satisfying added benefit.

While a mentor/mentee relationship can and does happen naturally in life, creating a framework that fosters these relationships can be extremely beneficial. This book is the story of designing programs introduced in schools and organizing a school-based mentoring program that provides opportunities for students to be mentored by caring adults. Mentoring is not to deal with a learning or discipline problem, but in the belief that a mentee would profit from the extra attention of a sensitive and caring adult. This is where the mentor comes in. *The key mentor qualification is a caring concern for those who are younger and a readiness to help them develop into the best person possible.*

Historically, intentional mentoring wasn't exactly necessary. The world was largely comprised of large, well-connected extended families in which supportive mentor/mentee relationships naturally existed. It was difficult to feel alone, unsupported, or disconnected when the family was always near at hand and everyone had a front seat as it handled family business.

That's not the way it is today. Even in the best of families, members can lead separate lives with little one-on-one reinforcement. Anyone can feel left out with the unintended consequence of missing out on the attention everyone needs. When that happens, people can withdraw and feel even more disconnected. It doesn't necessarily call for a professional counselor. What's needed is a mentor.

I've known Ken Black for over forty years. He has dedicated his life to service as a teacher, principal, pastoral assistant, and mentor. After a remarkable career in education and ministry, Ken Black found a new calling in school-based mentoring. He learned from the ground up and through his dedication has become an expert in this vocation.

Ken has received recognition for his work in mentoring. In 2006, the village of Roselle, Illinois, was awarded the Governor's Hometown Award for the community-based mentor program Ken started. In 2007, Ken received both the Seeds of Hope Award from Wheat Ridge Ministries and the Alumnus of the Year Award from Concordia University, Chicago, honors that came to him as a result of his leadership in mentoring. He also has been honored by multiple school districts for the positive impact he has made with his AIMS mentoring program.

As a result of the workshops Ken has presented, mentoring materials have been distributed to participants in twenty-six states and seven countries. Several mentoring programs have been built with the help of Ken's expertise. It has been a dream of his to write a book that can continue to foster the growth and outreach of something he so passionately believes in.

This is that book.

If you want to help today's young people by connecting with them in a disconnected world, keep turning the pages. Ken will share his story with you, remind you of the power of mentors, and show you the steps to take to either support or, if so led, create a mentoring program. By the end of this book, I believe you will conclude that the answer to the question, "Me, a mentor?" is a resounding . . . "Yes, Me!"

INTRODUCTION

ME A MENTOR?

Since you have chosen to open this book, I feel confident in saying that you value caring for people and serving them in times of need. You know that caring and serving are wonderful gifts we share with others and are demonstrated in many special ways. Do you belong to a community or church group providing care and support? Maybe you've collected items for your local food bank. Have you participated in a clothing drive, volunteered for lunch room duty at a school, or helped students with reading enrichment activities? Are you a driver for "Meals on Wheels"? Perhaps you willingly respond and assist when disasters strike to help victims pick up the pieces.

These and many more opportunities for service abound. But what if at least a portion of one's time had the possibility of multiplying the impact on an organization or community? If that happened, then a person's influence would not only be felt at a single time and place, but the impact would be expanded and perpetuated. In other words, wouldn't the act of guiding others to better ways of learning and growing lead to exponential growth in being able to share their gifts in the service of others?

This type of impact results from mentoring—the intentional investment in supporting another person through listening and/or providing guidance and modeling for their growth in a skill, mind-set, or lifestyle. Wonderful opportunities to care and serve are all around us—and mentoring is one of them. I have had many mentors over the years, and I have been a mentor to others. Each mentoring experience has had a positive impact on my life.

I didn't think much about intentional mentoring through the first seventy years of my life. But as I repositioned in my profession toward retirement, mentoring emerged as the way I could best serve others in my later years. I learned to embrace school-based mentoring because I had many mentors who guided me. This led me to think deeply about the need to support people of all ages through mentoring experiences.

In retrospect, I now understand that God was preparing me for my life's journey all through my "growing up" years. The residents of Arcadia, Indiana, my parents, my grandparents, my friends, and the church community of my youth all influenced me through the significant care and mentoring they provided me. These experiences of my youth still motivate me today in serving others through intentional mentoring.

Thanks for letting me share my story with you. Whether you are active in your local community, public school district, or a faith-based institution, or simply an individual interested in discovering what mentoring is all about, it is my hope that you will be encouraged to **BE** the mentor someone needs, whether they are a child, a parent, a student, a church member, a coworker, or a friend. The positive results of mentoring are life changing for both the mentor and the mentee.

Someone out there needs YOU!

Enjoy the journey!

Ken Black

CHAPTER ONE
WHY MENTORING MATTERS

"We live in a world in which we need to share responsibility. It's easy to say it's not my child, not my community, not my world, not my problem. Then there are those who see the need and respond. I consider these people my heroes."

~ Fred Rogers

Through the years, I have had a concern for young people who grow up lacking an effective support system. Who is going to talk to them? Who will listen to them? Who will inspire them? Who will support them? Who will be there to help guide them through tough decisions? I was very blessed in my formative years to have my own strong support system. This is part of my story of becoming active in the mentoring field. It includes a network of hundreds of people who, through the years, provided the love, patience, encouragement, and care I needed.

The stories I share here are just a few of the vivid memories

I still have of events and discussions with special people in different seasons of my life. Looking back, I can point to specific people and times when all the questions listed in the previous paragraph were answered for me. I see how blessed I was to have had an incredibly strong network of support and mentors, and how this ignited the desire in me to provide that same guidance for a child who may not have what I experienced.

My earliest mentors offered me the kind of support that I do not take for granted. It may have been a "different time" in history, but I was fortunate enough to have them to guide me along the way. And this journey began in a small, central Indiana town.

THE ARCADIA COMMUNITY AS MENTORS

For the first twenty years of my life—from the mid-1930s to the 1950s—I lived in Arcadia, Indiana. The population averaged about one thousand people. My home was a block from Main Street, and the shopping area was just three blocks long on both sides of the street. Our house had a front porch where our family gathered on warm summer evenings since there was no air-conditioning for those hot days of summer. In winter, the house was heated by a coal and wood burning furnace in the basement, and I often stood on the heat register in our dining room to get warm. The ping-pong room in the basement was one of my favorite places. We had some fierce ping-pong battles through the years with family and friends.

The Arcadia school system had only one building housing the elementary, junior high, and high school students. By attending a smaller school, I was able to play on the basketball team, had parts in plays and musicals, sang in the school choir, and played the bass drum in a band.

A strong sense of family permeated the community. In the farmland surrounding Arcadia, barns displayed the name of the owners and the year the family settled in the area. Several generations of the same family farmed the land for decades, passing down their views and values to their children and grandchildren. We were surrounded by family and friends and knew the names of our neighbors.

Families in Arcadia looked out for one another. I remember walking to Main Street for ice cream one hot, summer day. When I got my ice-cream cone, I teased the clerk and told her I understood the ice cream was free that day. I planned to play a little joke and pay her when I left the store. I forgot to pay her, and by the time I walked home, my mother had already received a phone call about the incident. I immediately went back to the ice-cream store with my money still in my pocket and apologized to the clerk. News gets around fast in a small town.

I belonged to the local 4-H club. I had 4-H leaders who taught me basic leadership and management skills. I learned lessons beyond farming, including how to plan and complete a project. I remember a meeting where a farmer talked about taking time before you begin a task to figure out the most efficient way to complete it. Sound time management advice!

I still like to walk through vegetable gardens and see the produce ripening. There is something about planting seeds and then waiting for the harvest that I have always enjoyed. I guess I have a few farming genes left in me.

When I drive through Arcadia today, I look for the ice-cream store, the brick Main Street structures, and the railroad crossing. I remember daily trains bringing mail and boxes from Sears Roebuck & Company to the small railroad depot in town. The house where I grew up is still there with another family making it their home.

I drive by the house I lived in every time I visit the Arcadia area. I still remember many of the names of the people who lived in our neighborhood. Why do I remember their names? I knew their families. I mowed many of their lawns. I was the backup paperboy for some of my friends who had paper routes. We also had neighbors who met together once a month at different homes to play euchre, a card game. They allowed young people to participate as soon as we could reasonably play the game. And the refreshments were always delicious because they were homemade.

Looking back, I was so very blessed to be raised in Arcadia, where the sense of community was strong and where residents looked after one another and sought to serve together. Unfortunately, most of our communities today do not have this same level of natural mentorship of others. As a result, there are gaps to be filled in leading and helping others grow.

PARENTS AS MENTORS

Not everyone is blessed with wonderful parents, but I sure was. They taught me so much about life and how to treat and love one another. They were extraordinary mentors to me.

My father, Guy Black, and my grandfather, Ira Black, operated a store in Arcadia. They sold groceries, meat, candy, dry goods, hardware, plumbing supplies, appliances, and a host of other items. It was truly a "general" store.

In the early 1940s, operating a general store became difficult. Meat, sugar, shoes, tires, and other items in short supply were rationed because of World War II. All available resources went to the war effort. Appliances were no longer manufactured. Both my father and grandfather had health issues, so they decided to close the store. They chose to auction off everything left in the store and then divided the proceeds equally among the seven churches in Arcadia. Why do I still remember this story? It is because my father and grandfather planted the seeds of cheerful giving in my heart.

After the general store closed, my grandfather retired, but my father continued to sell appliances and bottled gas, which were high pressure steel cylinders storing compressed fuel, used mainly in rural areas where natural gas was not available. When I got my driver's license, I delivered bottled gas to customers in a seven-mile radius from Arcadia. I also assisted Dad when he delivered appliances and hooked up gas stoves and water heaters.

One afternoon, I helped Dad install bottled gas at a home in the country. When we entered the house, I could tell the family, a young couple with three small children, was poor. The children's clothing was tattered, and they were not wearing shoes. When my father gave them the bill, I noticed he did not charge them for the installation of the stove, and the price of the bottled gas was much less than usual. In the truck on the way home, Dad explained to me that he just could not charge them the full price. He saw that the family was struggling financially, and he wanted to help others in need. This experience led me to consider how I could care for others who needed help.

Dad enjoyed life. He was a hard worker, but he also joked and laughed a lot. He took time to go hunting and fishing. He also tended to pull pranks on people. Some Sunday afternoons, my family visited friends unannounced. If our friends were not home, my father went into the house and rearranged the furniture. Back then, nobody locked their doors. When our friends came home, the family would step into their house, and right away, they knew Guy Black had been there!

Dad had expectations for me. He required me to listen to my mother and do what she asked me to do. When I had chores to complete, he insisted that I complete them before I went out to play. It was imperative for me to be home on time for dinner and to eat all the food on my plate. I understood my father's expectations, and I never doubted the high level of love and support he provided me.

My mother, Lucille, was a kind and caring person. I learned much from her about treating others with respect. When she heard harsh words about anyone, she softened her voice and let it be known that we are not judges. Mother had a multitude of friends. She was a great listener and helped her friends work through family issues. She provided meals to those who were sick. Since we lived two blocks from the railroad tracks, there were still those who rode the rails just after the Great Depression. No jobs were available, but men went from town to town riding in boxcars, looking for work. Every week or so, we had young men who came to our back door asking for a meal, and Mother always took time to feed them.

I will never forget Mother's routine when it was time for bed. She came to our upstairs bedroom to read a Bible story to my brother and me and to help us say our prayers. Sometimes, we could even talk her into reading a second story to us. This bedtime routine was an important part of my religious up-bringing, and I am so thankful to my mother for taking the time to read to us each evening.

My mother taught Sunday school until she was in her eight-ies. She also took time to teach Vacation Bible School each summer. In those days, Vacation Bible School lasted two weeks, so this was a real commitment of time to serve young people, but she did it because she really cared for them.

Mother had her own playful sense of humor. One Easter morning after she hid the Easter baskets outside, my brother, sister, and I ran out the back door to find our baskets. We all saw one Easter basket in plain sight in the middle of the backyard. We all ran to the basket—only to find there were no Easter eggs or candy in it. There was just a note that read, "April Fools." That year, Easter was on April 1st.

Later in life, after I had moved to Roselle, Illinois, Mother was so happy when my family drove to Arcadia for a visit. She kept a list of each grandchild's favorite foods and made sure to serve them during our visits. We always knew a meal would be ready regardless of the time we arrived. Our standard "coming home" meal was waffles and sausages. Mother had the waffle batter ready to put in the waffle iron as soon as we arrived.

Mother was a great encourager with a gentle spirit. When I made my choice to attend a college that was far from home, she supported my decision. She was devoted to our family, and I still marvel at how she managed the family's schedule so well—taking care of three children, working around Dad's changing schedule with long hours of work, having meals ready on time, and being involved in so many church and community activities. She was the kind of mother everyone should have. I thank God for the mother He provided for me. Her love and care for me never wavered.

When my brother Don, my sister Mary Ellen, and I talk about our parents, we each have our own special memories and stories to share, but we all come to the same conclusion: our parents were great gifts from God. They were effective mentors who provided a strong support system for us.

Back Row: Ken Black & Don Black
Front Row: Father Guy Black, Mother Lucille Black,
Sister Mary Ellen Black

Even in this era, there were many broken homes or dysfunctional circumstances where young people were living adrift from the bedrock of parental guidance. Today, it seems that this parental leadership is missing for even more young people. From whom will they learn the important lessons I learned from my parents?

GRANDPARENTS AS MENTORS

All four of my grandparents were alive until after I was a teenager. Because we lived close by, I was fortunate to be able to visit them often.

Grandpa and Grandma Black lived just a mile away from our home. Grandma Black always had homemade cookies in her cookie jar when we visited, and I could usually smell the aroma of the cookies when I entered the house.

I remember winter days when we went sledding on a hill near my grandparents' home. When we all came back to the house, Grandma insisted we put our gloves, hats, and coats near the stove to dry. She didn't want us to catch a cold. She also had hot chocolate waiting. Grandma Black took good care of us.

Another memorable experience comes from one Easter morning after our family attended a sunrise worship service. Once the service ended, we drove to my grandparents' home. They had a chicken house on their property, so we pulled a prank on them by placing colored Easter eggs in the chicken nests. It was great fun for us and enjoyable for Grandpa and Grandma Black too. I guess I could say that the surprises and gentle humor created healthy relationships in our family.

I also appreciated Grandpa and Grandma Black when I was a student at Concordia Junior College in Fort Wayne, Indiana. I realized one day that all my spending money was gone. This happened from time to time, but I could usually find a weekend job to earn extra cash. On that same day, Grandpa and Grandma Black sent me a ten-dollar bill as a surprise gift. To put the amount of this gift in proper perspective, think of it this way. A one-dip ice-cream cone cost five cents in those days. This was a great fortune and, to this day, I still remember receiving that letter and cash. Random acts of kindness were a way of life for my grandparents, and they provided this example for me to follow.

My Grandpa and Grandma Leininger, my mother's parents, lived on a farm seven miles north of Arcadia. Seeing them work the farm gave me an appreciation for hard labor and toil. I cannot comprehend how many hours Grandpa spent plowing, cultivating, and harvesting crops each year. In addition to milking cows twice each day, taking care of a large garden, raising pigs and chickens, mixing feed for the animals, plus myriad other tasks, he still carved out time to spend with me.

One afternoon, Grandpa Leininger asked me to help him milk the cows. I was afraid of them, and I couldn't get any milk in the bucket. It didn't take long for me to figure out that Grandpa had a gift for milking cows, and I didn't, but at least he gave me the chance to try something I had never done before.

I marveled at Grandpa's work ethic and his ability to teach me what farm life was like. To this day, I enjoy driving through agricultural areas, observing seasonal farm activities.

As for my Grandma Leininger, it seemed that she was always working in the kitchen. I still don't understand how she prepared such delicious meals for so many people using a wood burning stove. She was always busy with something, yet when my brother, sister, and I came running into the house for a cup of cold water, Grandma stopped what she was doing and pumped cool water from the well for us. Sometimes, she even gave us a cookie or a piece of candy. I think she was happy to see us because it gave her a little break in which to relax.

Summer was a busy time for Grandma Leininger. She canned a lot of food each summer. When the produce was ready to pick, my mother, brother, sister, and I all helped with the canning process. We took the husks and silks off the corn, and when the peas were harvested, we popped open the pea-pods and put *most* of the peas in a container. (Fresh peas are delicious!)

We had traditions in our family that created consistency. On Christmas Day, we always went to Grandpa and Grandma Black's house, and the Sunday after Christmas was always the gathering at Grandpa and Grandma Leininger's home. During the summer, family reunions were scheduled the same weekend year after year. When weddings or funerals took place, families came together to celebrate and to support one another.

Another routine I could depend upon was seeing my grandparents in church. All four grandparents embraced the same spiritual values. This common spiritual ground provided a solid base for my own spiritual nourishment.

I have great respect for my four grandparents as special mentors. Their clear-cut values of honesty, hard work, kindness, concern for others, and spiritual support were lessons I learned from them as I grew and matured. My grandparents were great mentors to me.

Unfortunately, because of our increasingly disconnected society and family groups, not everyone has strong grandparent mentors, and many miss out on the significant lessons that grandparents provide. Where will our youth today receive this special type of guidance from loving grandparents?

CHURCH MEMBERS AS MENTORS

Sunday morning was church day. This was a given. In addition to that, my family participated in many church activities throughout the year. Mother attended the monthly Ladies Aid meetings and taught Sunday school. My father was the church treasurer. My brother, sister, and I attended Sunday school, weekday confirmation classes, youth choir rehearsals, and youth meetings.

The Walther League was my church youth program where I attended monthly meetings. Our youth leaders led discussions on faith, giving, service, responsibility, and spiritual growth and provided time for fellowship. As we grew older, we helped plan our meetings, led discussion groups, and gave reports on upcoming youth activities.

A highlight for me each summer was our youth group outing to one of the Indiana State Parks, where we enjoyed hiking, crossing rivers, and seeing waterfalls. I'm glad we had a core group of parents and friends who took time to plan and chaperone these trips. These chaperones were role models for me. I appreciate their willingness to put up with me and other youth on a day trip to a different state park year after year.

Years later, I continued to receive support from my church family. My wife, Marcia, died from fast-spreading cancer in October of 2004. Members of my home congregation, Trinity Lutheran

Church, brought meals to our home each day when Marcia was in hospice care and were quick to respond when I needed help. I remember one evening when Marcia requested a bottle of 7-Up, and we didn't have any in the fridge. My neighbors were not home, so I called a church member who lived several blocks away. He immediately went to the store and dropped off six bottles of 7-Up at our house. He later thanked me for allowing him to help out. This spirit of giving prevailed in my church homes, both as a youth and as an adult.

A sad reality today is that not everyone is a part of a church family. As church attendance ebbs, fewer people are impacted by church members. The lessons of service to others and faith are not as easily transferred as a result.

How do I know mentoring matters? I know so because I was effectively mentored in so many ways by such a wide variety of people in Arcadia. I did not realize it at the time, but in my early years, God was actively molding me and preparing me for future service.

What about you? What are the gifts and talents you have been given for serving others? As God prepared me, through the type of childhood I experienced, to mentor others, you may also have been prepared to meet the needs of others—to serve as a mentor in some way, to provide guidance to another, or simply to lend a sympathetic listening ear.

While my Arcadia years were so important in preparing me to be a mentor, I did not realize their significance for many years. It was not until I was charged with the challenge of leading the ministry to seniors at the church where I served that I would be led to explore the potential blessings of intentional mentoring. I remain thankful for this mentoring I received in my formative years.

I hope these personal experiences have helped build the case that various types of mentoring are desperately needed in our communities today. But what are some practical ways you can be that significant mentor in the lives of others? Continue this journey with me, and you will discover how you, too, can make a difference in this disconnected world.

CHAPTER TWO

THE AIMS STORY

"Never doubt that a small group of thoughtful, committed citizens can change the world. Indeed, it's the only thing that ever has."

~ Margaret Mead

As I dreamed about authoring the book you have in your hands, it became clear that God led me on a very specific journey to reach the point where learning to be a mentor and empowering others to become mentors was a significant part of my life. Perhaps the most important element of this journey was the establishment of an organization named AIMS. I want to share with you the story of AIMS. I do this not out of ego or the expectation that each reader will choose to mentor others by building a similar program, but so that one can detect the path on which God led me to understand better how to mentor others and to communicate the importance of mentoring to those in my sphere of influence. Perhaps you may see a glimpse of how God has been leading you through this journey as well.

———∼∼∼———

So what is AIMS? And what does this term have to do with mentoring? AIMS is the acronym chosen for a school-based mentor program that began in Roselle, Illinois, in 2003. AIMS stands for *Adults Involved in Mentoring Students.* Over time, students in fourteen area schools benefited from the mentoring provided through AIMS. I had the privilege of organizing and coordinating AIMS for nearly a decade.

As I look back, I did not realize this at the time, but God was preparing me for mentoring work with AIMS in the years that preceded the establishment of the organization. There were many links between individuals that needed to be established before AIMS could be a reality. This began with my upbringing in Arcadia, Indiana, and continued as I pursued a vocation in education. As I grew in my chosen profession, I saw firsthand the many needs of children, which often were difficult to meet within a traditional classroom. Transitioning to church administration in the late 1970s, I became aware of other mentoring necessities in both a church congregation and the surrounding community. Finally, as I was nearing the traditional age of retirement, I discovered the power of school-based mentoring approaches. It was time for AIMS to be born, and that happened without fanfare in February 2003.

If I had not been a teacher, I doubt if there would have been an AIMS organization. It so happened that when I was in fourth grade, I knew nothing about mentoring, but I wanted to be a teacher. How did I know? I just did! That's all I can say! It may sound like this was too early in life to make a career choice, but I don't ever remember considering any other vocation. My twenty-three years of teaching experience provided the validation that having mentors for students would provide an additional layer of needed support for these children as they grew and matured.

I chose to attend Concordia Teachers College (now Concordia University, Chicago) located in River Forest, Illinois, to become a teacher. I graduated from Concordia with a Bachelor of Science Degree in Education and a Master of Arts Degree in Education. I was ready to begin my teaching career.

I believe my role in founding AIMS started on the first day I stepped into my classroom and greeted my students. This took place in 1955. I dreamed of being a teacher, and there I was, greeting third-, fourth-, and fifth-graders in my classroom in a three-room Lutheran school in Tipton, Indiana. I was elated but also a little scared. Like most who embark on a new opportunity, I wondered if I would be up to the challenge of becoming an effective teacher. "How do I teach three different classes in one classroom?" I asked myself. When I began teaching, I realized that my students had already adapted to this teaching model because of their previous years in the school. It was I who had to adjust.

There was one big factor that aided me in providing instruction for three different grades in my classroom. I had opted to enroll in my student teaching class the summer before my first year of teaching. My student teaching experience was in a multigrade classroom at Immanuel Lutheran School in Elmhurst, Illinois. I was able to glean many ideas on classroom management from a master teacher, Mr. Moderow, a teacher at the Lutherbrook Children's Center in Addison, Illinois, during my time under his tutelage.

For the first few days in working with Mr. Moderow, I observed how he easily moved to work with different grades within his multigrade classroom and how he combined classes for certain academic subjects, when appropriate. He seemed always to have students engaged in learning activities, whether it was within a class session or as homework. I met with Mr. Moderow each day, and we had many conversations about the teaching techniques that worked in the multigrade setting. He also patiently suggested additional teaching methods for me to try. In retrospect, I can now see how this master teacher actively mentored me. He was an incredible encourager, and I quickly understood that my students needed the same type of encouragement from me as I received from my supervising teacher.

I discovered the importance of seeing each student as an individual during that first year of teaching. While classrooms at this time typically used only group instruction models, I noticed the positive benefits of connecting with a student one-on-one whenever possible. Students need the undivided attention of their teacher even if it is just a personal "Hello" or a "High Five." Clearly, teachers become a natural part of a student's support system.

Sometimes, I saw students who needed extra attention while others completed their homework quickly. How does an educator deal with this? It was a balancing act! When students had time on their hands, they were eager to assist those students who needed extra help—a natural mentoring opportunity! I now realize that each learning experience I had in teaching was a building block for my foundation in understanding the value of providing a strong support system for students. My first year of teaching went well.

I served in other ways as a member at the Tipton church that year. I played the organ for the Sunday worship service every other week. This was an expected duty for a teacher graduating from Concordia in 1955. I helped with the church youth group, coached a basketball team, and was in charge of the hot lunch program at the school. What a juggling act! I was learning to manage the responsibilities that were assigned to me. I was pleased with this beginning step on my educational journey. And, yes, I did have fun playing softball, basketball, and other games at recess and lunch hour with my students.

The next year, I moved to Elmhurst, Illinois, where I taught seventh-graders for two years at Immanuel Lutheran School. One grade! One room! Older students! At this grade level, students were more independent. There were more cliques. New friendships were made while other friendships disintegrated. It was evident that students were seeking their own identity. While the idea of mentors for students had not yet emerged, I began to realize that some students needed more adult support in their life. In addition, working with another age group of students and understanding their needs and issues better prepared me for working with middle school students within the AIMS program.

In 1958, I moved on to Immanuel Lutheran School in Hillside, Illinois, where I not only served as principal, but I also taught a classroom of fifth- through eighth-graders my first year. Our school was selected by Concordia Teachers College, my alma mater, as a training ground for student teachers. Our entire staff became role models for these fledgling educators. More opportunities for mentoring!

In the summer of 1966, I became the principal of Trinity Lutheran School in Roselle, Illinois, and served in this role for twelve years. This was a larger school where more administrative work was necessary. Time was needed for meeting with parents and school board members, budget preparation, public relations work, committee meetings, conference attendance, staff meetings, fire drills, attending athletic events, scheduling sessions, and the creation and distribution of many reports.

All of this administrative work allowed me to meet with many people one-on-one as well as in group settings. A large variety of topics was discussed in these sessions. Learning how to be a good listener, to ask for clarification, to be able to share alternative suggestions, to affirm good ideas, and to put people at ease when talking with them, served to build a skill set that would later be essential in helping establish AIMS. Practicing these aptitudes as principal prepared me for the many future meetings with local school administrators, community leaders, and teachers when mentoring was considered in Roselle area schools through AIMS.

Looking back, my experiences in education made it possible for me to start and coordinate a mentor program. Even if I had not been led to start a mentor program, I know I would have been an eager recruit to serve as a mentor.

I first heard about school-based mentoring programs in 1992, from Carol Gienapp, a cousin of my wife, Marcia. Every three years Carol and Gary Gienapp hosted a family reunion in Chippewa Falls, Wisconsin. One year, Carol talked about a new venture in which she was involved. Her new role was being the first paid coordinator of a mentor program in Chippewa Falls. At future reunions, Carol continued to update the relatives on the program's progress, and her enthusiasm showed me how much she enjoyed her work.

As my career in education progressed, I served as a Lutheran school principal for many years. Based on what I saw as a principal, I knew a mentor program was a good idea that would benefit my students, though I did not have time to pursue it initially. As I look back now, my interest was piqued by Carol's work and passion for her role in Wisconsin. I had no idea that several years later, I would have an opportunity to start a mentor program in my community.

After twenty-three years of teaching and serving as a principal, I transitioned to the role of administrative assistant to
the pastor at Trinity Lutheran Church in Roselle, Illinois,
where I worked closely with Rev. Charles Mueller Sr. I enjoyed serving in this role for many years. When I turned
sixty-five, I decided to serve part time. By then, Pastor
Mueller's son was the new senior pastor of the church. Rev.
Charles Mueller Jr. asked me to lead and coordinate programs and activities for the senior adult ministry.

This was the perfect challenge for me. I was already a senior,
so I could identify most of my contemporaries by name. I
knew some of the joys and heartaches our seniors had experienced, and I appreciated them for their commitment to serve
others in the church and community. I was ready and willing
to begin this new phase of service.

I talked with a few seniors and asked if they would serve on
the new Senior Adult Ministry committee. We chose a new
name for our group, JOY. I liked the name because it is based
on Psalm 126:3, "The Lord has done great things for us, and
we are filled with JOY."

It didn't take long for JOY to get to work making some
important decisions. The committee understood the value
seniors bring to a church and community, so we asked ourselves, "What can we do to increase the number of opportunities seniors have for caring and serving?" While fellowship
among group members was important, it was clear to me
that this group craved a meaningful purpose beyond simply
existing as a social group.

The JOY committee decided to spend six months exploring opportunities for seniors to use their gifts and abilities in service to others more effectively. As this process progressed, I recalled the work of Carol Gienapp and her passion for mentoring. It seemed that God had led us to the right time to act. I put mentoring on the agenda for our next ministry meeting. At this meeting, I told everyone about Carol and her role with the Chippewa Area Mentor Program. Even though there were many questions, I could sense a positive enthusiasm for a mentor program and that people were intrigued by the possibility of starting one of our own.

A committee member suggested we plan a trip to Chippewa Falls to observe their mentor program to give us a better grasp on how the program functioned. A small contingent of us made the journey on what turned out to be a life-changing trip.

Carol Gienapp was the master planner for our three-day visit. She invited us to meet with a small group of community leaders to talk about the Chippewa Area Mentor Program. The enthusiasm of our new Chippewa Falls friends about the need for mentoring was a sure sign to me that their mentor program was important to them and the community. At the time of our visit, they had over 200 adults of all ages mentoring 260 students. Even with this sizeable number of mentors involved, there was still a waiting list of 170 students who needed mentors. Obviously, the program had identified and addressed a significant need.

On the first day of our visit, we spent time visiting two

schools to observe mentors working with their mentees. In one mentor session I witnessed, the dialog between the mentor and her mentee was so focused, they didn't notice I was in the room. In another session, the mentor included me in the conversation. When the mentee found out why I was visiting, he said, "I like it. I like my mentor. You should get one [a mentor program] started!"

It was a pleasure to see mentors and students genuinely enjoy conversing with one another. I talked with one mentor who worked with ten different students and was at school each day of the week. Mentoring children became his passion after he retired. Another mentor was a retired schoolteacher. She missed her students but enjoyed the different pace of life in retirement. Being a mentor gave her a sense of fulfillment, knowing she could still work with a young student who needed a special friend. These conversations showed our group that mentoring could fit the lifestyles of retirees in a variety of ways.

On our second day, we met with mentors, teachers, social workers, and principals. One social worker explained that because of the mentor program, fewer students needed her assistance. She said she could now spend more time with those students who needed more care. A mentor commented that she looked forward to her visit with her mentee each week as it was the highlight of her week. One principal had high praise for what the mentor program was accomplishing. Students gained self-esteem and interacted with classmates better than before they had a mentor—an amazing transformation! This day was impactful for our group. The practical elements of a school-based mentoring program were unclear until we saw this type of intentional mentoring in action. We certainly came away with a better understanding of what school-based mentoring was all about and how this might meld with the mission of JOY.

My wife, Marcia, having served as an elementary school teacher before the birth of our children, also recognized the value of one-on-one mentoring. Being able to focus on just one person at a time allowed better communication between a mentor and the mentee. We enjoyed the no-pressure, easy-paced atmosphere in the room when these meetings took place. It was amazing to me that we didn't hear anything negative about the Chippewa Falls Mentor Program during our three-day observation.

On the last morning of our visit, Carol gave us a copy of their mentor handbook, various administrative forms, and suggestions for mentoring activities. We now had mentor materials to review and observations to share with the JOY group when we returned to Roselle.

Driving back to Roselle from Chippewa Falls, our committee discussed our next step. It was quite clear to each of us that the mentor program we had seen was well-organized and was embraced by the community. We were impressed with the remarkable work being accomplished by the many volunteer mentors serving the students in Chippewa Falls. We decided to recommend to JOY that we move ahead to determine whether there was a need for a similar program in

Roselle and assess the potential for the acceptance of a new start-up mentor program in our area. The full Senior Adult Ministry committee accepted the recommendation. We were ready and anxious to get started.

For our group of seniors, there was a *right time* for them to be ready and willing to become mentors in our local community schools. On a personal level, there was a *right time* for me to get involved in school-based mentoring. My *right time* did not come until I was sixty-nine years old, but through God's guidance and the planning and preparation He provided me through the years, it did come!

While an intentional school-based mentoring program is only one way in which mentoring may be established, this type of outreach has proven to be a significant blessing in Roselle and many other communities. There are many approaches to mentoring that we will explore together. Some of these methods are highly organized. Other mentoring opportunities occur organically or in much smaller settings. Before we review the variety and scope of mentoring activities, allow me to share some larger lessons from the school-based mentoring program of AIMS, of which I was privileged to found and lead.

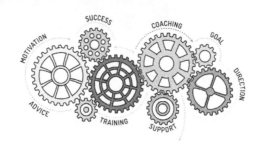

CHAPTER THREE

SCHOOL-BASED MENTORING

"I believe so much in mentoring and the incredible impact it can have on youth today. I have never witnessed a more powerful intervention for making a difference in the lives of young people. In my mind, it does not get any better than matching a child with a caring individual to provide him or her with support, competence, character, direction, and a chance for a productive life."

~ Dr. Susan G. Weinberger
From *Mentoring a Movement—
My Personal Journey*

Still with me? I sure hope so! Perhaps after reading the previous chapter, you are thinking, "Well, a large program like that found in Chippewa Falls or with AIMS sounds great, but I don't know if that is for me." No problem! Not everyone is called to be a program creator. However, if you are even a bit curious about how a school-based mentoring program might be formed, this is the chapter for you. And even if you have no interest in building a program, one can still find an existing program in which to serve, investing as little as an hour a week. While school-based mentoring programs are not the only path for serving as a mentor (in fact, we will explore many more mentoring models in Chapter Four), the power of mentoring students within their existing schools is significant.

As I shared earlier, I have been blessed with a great number of people in my life who have been a part of my support system—who have intentionally mentored me through the years. Call them friends, family, neighbors--in many ways, these mentors guided me on my spiritual journey and up-lifted me when I struggled.

But not everyone has the benefit and blessing of a stable, loving, extended family—and even if they do, the children of today's world need every bit of support and guidance they can get. The world today is far different from the one than the one in which I grew up. The pace of the world is faster, more distracted, and people are becoming more and more disconnected from one another.

I believe you already know this. You picked up this book for a reason. You have a heart to serve and want to do more in your community.

The need for mentors is great. Perhaps that is why once I learned about school-based mentoring, I knew I wanted to be a part of it—and ultimately, AIMS was established. If you are ready to participate in a mentor program, but none exist in your area, you too can build your own program.

Since we launched a successful program after much investigation and exploration, it is my hope my journey might serve as a guide for the establishment of other mentor programs, sharing insights concerning the necessary steps to embark on your own journey in creating a program or joining an existing program.

In this chapter, we'll review the "requirements" to be a good mentor, how to find a program, and—of course—how to build one if no program exists!

HOW DO I BECOME A MENTOR?

The Chippewa Falls, Wisconsin, Mentor Program created this "job description" of a mentor. Other programs may define a mentor in different ways. I challenge you to consider whether you possess the characteristics necessary to support students in a formal, school-based mentoring process.

Purpose:

To develop a positive relationship with a young person (grade K–12) that will advance the student's social development and emotional growth.

Responsibilities:

- Meeting with a mentee for thirty minutes every week
- Developing a personal and positive rapport with a child
- Acting as cheerleader, coach, and advocate for children
- Maintaining ongoing contact with the school counselor and Mentor Program Coordinator, sharing concerns, highlights, and ideas
- Sharing your knowledge, experiences, and interests

Qualifications:

- Enjoy working with children
- Basic friendship skills such as being reliable, accepting, listening, and suggesting
- Positive attitude
- Passion for advocating the success of youth
- Flexibility
- Ability to accept children as they are
- Ability to maintain confidentiality

Requirements:

- Submit an application with references
- Pass background checks
- Meet with Mentor Program Staff for an in-person interview/training
- Be emotionally stable and mature

Benefits:

- Personal fulfillment through contribution to an individual and the community
- Satisfaction in helping someone mature, progress, and achieve goals
- Networking with other community members
- Training sessions which are offered regularly for the volunteer's personal growth and development
- Mentee/Mentor group events

One of my professional mentors, Pastor Charles Mueller Sr., describes a mentor's role in this way:

To serve in that role, you will need to relax, open yourself to your mentee, and help them become the finest human being possible. To do this, it will help if you are ready to do the following things:

- Be an active, attentive listener. Attentive means focusing on them and their expressed needs when together. Active means helping them clarify what they are trying to say while showing concern and giving the best guidance of which you are capable. Your goal is to help them make the key life discoveries as painlessly as possible, and this will help them make it on their own.
- Answer questions. Answer them as fully as the circumstance allows while also pointing them to others like a parent, a teacher, or another friend, who can help. While doing this, make it clear that you don't know all the answers, nor do you feel this is a weakness.

- Strive to react thoughtfully. Ask questions, both for your benefit and for that of your mentee. Help them clarify their concerns as best you can.
- Be wary of offering unsolicited advice. As so often happens at every level of life, the longer we talk about a subject, the more likely an excellent solution will surface almost of itself, with but a little intentional or even unintentional guidance. Help the mentee own not only the question but also the answer.
- Give deserved affirmation. We all bloom under affirmation. Take the time to state—and even restate—to your mentee all positive signs you see. Nothing false and no flattery, but try to share encouraging words whenever you can.
- The goal is to be a good, older friend. You may be the first older friend your mentee has ever had, so . . . lay a good foundation on which to build.

Do you meet these criteria? Well, then—let's get started!

HOW TO BEGIN MENTORING WHEN A SCHOOL-BASED MENTORING PROGRAM ALREADY EXISTS

Some schools and school districts already have mentor programs in place. Call the receptionist or volunteer coordinator at your local school. If they have a mentor program, schedule a meeting with the staff person who coordinates the mentor program.

After meeting with the mentor coordinator, attend a mentor training class. The mentor trainer will talk about the specifics of mentoring in a school setting, and you should come away with a better understanding of their expectations and the mentoring experience. If you still are not sure about being a mentor, ask to shadow a mentor during a mentoring session. This firsthand experience may give you new insights.

Once you have gone through this process, you are ready to make a choice: *Say yes to mentoring, maybe later,* or *no.* All three of these answers are legitimate. If it is not the right time for you to start mentoring, that is fine. However, if you choose to make a personal commitment to move forward, you will embark on a journey which will be a life-changer for you and your mentee.

ARE THERE OPPORTUNITIES TO MENTOR IN SCHOOLS WHERE THERE IS NO FORMAL MENTORING PROGRAM?

If there are no mentor programs in the schools in your surrounding area and you feel the call to help students, there are additional avenues to explore (from my own experience) for opportunities to care for and serve young people.

If you want to assist teachers and students in a school setting, call the school receptionist at your neighborhood school and ask about volunteer opportunities. It would be helpful if you could also share the type of volunteer work you would like to do. Some of these volunteer activities may include helping with art projects, providing support for reading and math classes, or even helping on vision screening and school picture days.

Never underestimate the value of your volunteer service. A conversation with a student or teacher provides a link to further conversations. Your relationship with the student or teacher will blossom the more you volunteer. This gives you a chance to be a role model and a trusted friend of a student.

Teachers and staff members appreciate any kind of service you can provide, whether it is done only once or multiple times. The more you volunteer, the better you will understand how important you are to the educational process.

When I moved to Huntley, Illinois, I saw an announcement in a local newspaper requesting volunteers to help with the CARE Initiative at Martin Elementary School. Community Assistance for Reading Enrichment (CARE) was a third-, fourth-, and fifth-grade instructional model to work with students to enhance their reading skills. Volunteers come to the school once a week for an hour for five weeks and discuss one topic per visit.

I attended an orientation session led by the principal and then volunteered three different times for CARE. In one of my sessions, I learned from a student that there are more than two thousand species of fireflies. There is a Firefly Festival in the Smoky Mountains each summer. Did you know there are no fireflies in Europe? Fascinating!

One volunteer project may lead to others. One year, I received a call from the volunteer coordinator of my local school district, asking if I could come to school once a week and help four students with math, and I agreed. Teaching math has changed since I taught it fifty years ago. The four students had a better grasp of "new math" than I did. I survived because I had the answer chart that helped me work through the process of getting the right answers. Even with the challenge of not being fully prepared, it was still a good experience . . . and I probably learned more than the students did.

Two additional opportunities to volunteer in local schools came my way. One morning, I interviewed ten students who were applying for a job as a part of a study unit on job interviews. I met with each student for about fifteen minutes. Each one gave me their typed résumé, and I asked questions about their experience in their field of work, from babysitting to mowing lawns.

Another time, I was asked to be one of four judges for two book writing classes. Each student submitted a short book they had written, and the judges had to select the best book from each class. We had forty books to review. There are some great young authors out there!

The point in these examples is to show you that there are plenty of other opportunities to help schoolchildren if no mentoring program exists and you are not ready to begin your own. If you have a heart to help and you contact your local school and express an interest in volunteering, chances are they will have something for you to do!

Keep in mind that you will most likely have to go through a vetting process that includes a background check, but once you have completed those requirements, you will be able to volunteer in many different ways.

WHAT IF NO MENTORING PROGRAM EXISTS? BUILD ONE!

If you are ready to be a mentor, but there is no school-based program available to you, another powerful alternative is to build one.

This may seem like an overwhelming task. Start small! A mentor program can begin with just one match. You can be the mentor and have one mentee. The mentor program can grow one mentor/mentee match at a time.

If you decide to start a mentor program, I strongly urge you to visit a school or school district that has a successful mentor program. You will come away from your visit with enthusiasm and a deep appreciation for the value of mentoring.

When beginning your journey, you may need to convince your local school's faculty and/or administrators that a mentoring program will provide valuable benefits to students. Reviewing specific questions and their potential answers with your local school might be helpful at this point. Will mentoring add value to the educational and maturing processes for students? Will parents understand the importance of having mentors for their children? Will teachers and administrators support school-based mentor programs in their schools and districts?

These questions are not easy to answer. In some schools, it may take time to build a case for making mentors available for students in schools. In other schools, teachers and administrators understand the importance of mentoring, but no one has stepped up with a plan for implementing a mentoring strategy in their school. Perhaps you are being called and led to be this person.

A successful mentor program is defined less by the number of participants but more fully by the manner in which it meets the specific needs within a school and community. In addition, success is also seen in consistency and sustainability—something that is designed for long-term activity. Before we get into the steps to building a successful school-based mentoring program, let's first take a closer look at another program—the one that AIMS has its roots in—the Chippewa Area Mentor Program.

The Chippewa Area Mentor Program is an example of a mentor program that is sustainable. Why has it lasted so long? To find the answer to this question, I asked the Rev. Roger Skatrud, one of its founding members, to share his story of how mentoring became the focus of an entire community as an outreach to the youth in Chippewa Falls, Wisconsin. It took creative people with a passion for helping students to set in motion a well-organized plan for their mentor program—and their plan really worked. The Chippewa Area Mentor Program has continued to provide dedicated mentors for young people for over a quarter of a century in the Chippewa Falls area. Some crucial decisions in the early stages of development provided the foundation for this lasting entity. I appreciate the mind-set of those who organized this mentor program in Chippewa Falls and for their willingness to share their mentor program with others. The AIMS Mentor Program was a grateful recipient of this part of their plan as well, and now it can be yours, too.

Here is Roger's story:

A SUSTAINABLE MENTOR PROGRAM
by Roger Skatrud

"The Chippewa Area Mentor Program, in partnership with the community, is committed to strengthening students' social and emotional growth through one-on-one matching with caring and responsible role models."

~ Chippewa Area Mentor Program
Mission Statement

In June of 1988, the Board of Deacons and Social Ministries from Our Saviour's Lutheran Church in Chippewa Falls, Wisconsin, discussed ways for its members to reach out in service to the needs of the community. One person at this meeting pointed to the middle school across the street and said, "Maybe we should start by finding out if we can do something for our neighbors over there." Tom Welch, the middle school principal, had a dream of providing mentors for some of the students in his school—the soil was fertile and ready to bring forth a wonderful plant.

Two members from Our Saviour's made contact and visited Tom. At the July board meeting at Our Saviour's, they reported Tom's expressed interest in the possibility of getting help for students who were falling through the cracks and not thriving in their schoolwork. These students had no program in the curriculum to help them.

Tom had been trying to help students by using teachers and aides but felt it would be better to find help for these students outside the school staff. He made it clear that what was needed was not another teacher in the student's life but someone who would be a good listener.

In October of 1988, a plan was forged to assemble a committee in November that included board members of Our Saviour's, members of the church who work with children, and representatives from the middle school. The group would explore various ways for helping these *children of promise* who needed a special friend and role model.

It took several months of planning to prepare for the launching of the mentor program that met the needs of those children of promise. One discussion included what the relationship between the student and the adult should be called. It was decided to stay away from the terminology of a teacher, counselor, or tutor. After much discussion, the word *mentor* as the most appropriate term for the name of the adult who worked with the student was agreed upon.

Another decision was to maintain mentoring as a program of the community rather than a program of the school. If the school district assumed total responsibility for the program, they feared it would get lost in the many programs and concerns of the district. This community approach enabled the recruiting of mentors through community churches, service clubs, industry, senior citizen groups, and the business community. The strength of the mentor program became its wide volunteer base of mentors who provided wise and dependable role models for hundreds of students.

We next formed a mentor committee to promote, guide, and provide oversight of the program. They held monthly meetings at the middle school where the school counselors worked closely with them and identified students who could be helped by having a mentor. The school counselors then contacted the parents of these students and explained that a mentor could be provided for their son or daughter if they would give permission. With the permission of the parents, students were matched with adult volunteers, and a time during the school day was established for the pair to meet. It was in the second semester of the '88–'89 school year when the first six mentor-mentee matches began meeting. The choice to make the mentor program school-based, along with the cooperation of the teachers, counselors, and administration, solidified it as an effort of the community.

Some special fun events started to take place. In 1990, the program held its first mentor Spring Party at the middle school. The mentees proudly hosted the event which recognized the mentors. They also had a holiday pizza party at Our Saviour's Lutheran Church in December of 1991, with one hundred mentors and students present. Over the years, these two gatherings of mentors and mentees became a highlight for all participants. Pictures of the mentor pairs were taken and shared. These photos were also put up on a bulletin board in the mentor meeting rooms.

In November of 1990, the mentor program began its expansion to area elementary schools to meet the obvious need of providing mentoring at an earlier age. Mentors were eventually assigned to kindergarten students as well as older students. Some of these matches continued to meet year after year, providing stability for the students.

The program appealed to the community and the school district for monetary support. The school district provided significant "in kind" support, but they could not provide financial support. The community businesspeople, service clubs, individuals, and Our Saviour's Lutheran Endowment Fund, however, gave significant support. Eventually, the Chippewa Falls School District was able to provide funds for the program.

In 1991, the Chippewa Falls School District Superintendent and the Board of Education embraced the mentor program for its importance to the community. By the fall of 1992, it became clear that the coordination of the program was asking too much for the counselors and volunteers to administer. There was a need for someone to be available to provide outreach to the community and organize the mentor matches and events. As a result, Carol Gienapp became the first paid coordinator of the mentor program.

In 1993, bylaws were adopted that described the structure of the Chippewa Area Mentor Program and a Community Board. They provided for a board of ten members elected to a three-year alternating term. It was determined that the Community Board would include a mentor, school administrator, two school guidance counselors, a community business or organization representative, a church lay representative, clergy, and three community members-at-large.

Annual meetings took place and provided the ideal platform for communication to any who were interested in learning more about this unique community outreach, along with a review of the mentor program. The agenda included the election of members to three-year terms to the board, statistical reports on the current number of mentor-mentee matches, and the number of students who were still waiting for a mentor. Any questions were answered, as well. All of this communication and information solidified the program's connection to the community.

The very competent community relations board has maintained the credibility of the mentor program over many years. It has put in place the necessary guidelines for monitoring and overseeing the mentoring initiative. What makes the board strong is that it includes community leaders and representatives from the schools who are in touch with the work of the mentor.

This community relations board also has the responsibility of acting as a personnel committee. They determine the remuneration and hiring of the coordinators. They are responsible for the expenditure of funds for the various programs for the mentor activities. The funds are administered from the school district treasury at the direction of those who work for the mentor program. We were sensitive to the need for providing information about the mentoring program to all who provided support. From the beginning, we were careful of insurance liability issues to protect the mentors, the board, and the school district.

The mentor program's impact has been outstanding. In 2003, it was estimated that nearly five hundred mentors had served over one thousand students. The estimated "gift" of volunteer dollars to the school district approached $145,000. (I can't imagine what those figures would be now.)

Along with the benefit to students, those involved in mentoring have received rich rewards for what they have accomplished, too. Who wouldn't want to be a key player in the growth and maturity of a student who really needs extra attention? Mentors may not realize the importance of their mentoring at first, but talking to your mentee later in life will open your eyes to the unquestionable support you have provided.

———⌇⌇⌇———

Roger is a lifelong supporter of mentoring and remains involved in this important work to this day. He and many others made it possible for thousands of children to be supported by caring adults by sharing their mentor program with educators throughout Wisconsin and other states.

Vision, passionate leadership, creative planning, focus, strong community, and school support . . . These are just a few words that describe the success of the Chippewa Area Program, helping students for thirty years.

Does this vision and passion for mentoring create an interest in you for this type of organization? Perhaps you are then ready to work through the steps of building a mentor program within your community. As we review the suggested steps for such a process, please do not think you need to create a program as big as either the AIMS or Chippewa Falls programs. The scope of the program can be on a much-smaller scale to start with . . . and then who knows where it might take you and your community!

BUILDING A COMMUNITY-BASED MENTORING PROGRAM

Starting a mentor program is no easy task. While I had the enthusiasm and support of our JOY group, there were still many pieces we needed to put into place before we could make our vision a reality.

If you are not a part of an organization like I was, you will need to decide either to create the program on your own or to assemble a group of like-minded people who are ready to team up with you. For me, since I was the coordinator of the Senior Adult Ministry at Trinity Lutheran Church,

I first needed to get the approval and support of the senior pastor.

I shared with him our experience and insights from our trip to Chippewa Falls and explained that I felt this was a great way for our seniors to care and serve in the community and share their experiences with schoolchildren. After hearing me out, he said, "Go for it!"

I then volunteered to talk with school administrators in the area to garner interest in starting a mentor program. I was fortunate that I didn't have to start from scratch because Carol Gienapp and Chippewa Falls had generously supplied me with numerous mentor materials to guide my presentations. (NOTE: The link for the Chippewa Falls mentor handbook is found in the resources shared in Chapter Six.) I soaked up as much mentor information as I could to present to school personnel. I knew I needed to be ready when I met with school administrators to address their questions and concerns.

I started right within my Trinity community and made my initial presentation to Reed Sander, who was the current principal of Trinity Lutheran School. After consideration, Reed was my first administrator to say "yes" to mentoring.

What followed were several more school contacts and conversations—and several more "yesses." These schools agreed to listen to my presentation, and as I hope you will also experience, I received encouraging support. And this support had a ripple effect. Our local high school superintendent not only was eager to begin, but he also networked with other superintendents, and soon I was making presentations to those schools, too. Because I had attended mentor/mentee sessions while visiting Chippewa Falls, I had a clear understanding of how a mentor program works and was able to use this knowledge, along with gleaning information from the Chippewa Falls mentor handbook, to build these presentations. It is unlikely that these sessions would have been effective without a personal visit to view an effective mentoring program.

When I introduced the concept of mentoring to teachers, they had many questions. However, before long, they were asking when the mentor program would start. It was an easy sell to teachers when they began focusing on individual students in their classrooms who would benefit from having a mentor. They understood the need for additional adult support for their students. If you can help them think through the individual needs of their students, they will most likely be on board as you try to make a case for the program.

I share these experiences with you so that you might be better prepared for the challenges you are likely to encounter. Obviously, your path to share a vision may be different for each community and school, but it is always useful to learn from those who have previously experienced this process.

And my experience with school administrators has also proven to me that they, too, will see the value of mentoring. Here are some insights from district and school-level administrators that are typical of the reactions I received when making mentor program proposals:

Too few students have meaningful daily conversations with their parents. Too many parents are unable to schedule significant one-to-one time with their children. School, childhood, and adolescence are tough for too many students. Given these facts, school-based mentoring programs can fill an important void in reaching students academically in school.

I have observed and participated in school-based mentoring programs as both a middle school principal and a superintendent. Yes, these experiences were personally rewarding, but more importantly, they helped the growth, learning, and development of young people. I witnessed many youngsters who had much improved school experiences due to the attention from and contact with adult mentors.

The research is clear. Students who connect with a significant adult at school who really knows and cares about them are much more likely to experience success in school. My experience and observations further convince me of this.

~ Kim M. Perkins, Ed.D.
Retired Superintendent, Bloomingdale School
District #13, Bloomingdale, Illinois

Mentoring is truly a win-win. The idea of mentoring was to meet the needs of a student who may be new to the school, struggling with a loss, or having difficulty making friends. The truth of the matter is that time, and time again, the mentor feels that he or she reaps the benefits of mentoring just as much as the mentee does. All humans value relationships, and no matter what our age, we enjoy having someone in our life who is on our side, who is in our court. That's what mentoring is. Over the years, I had many mentors, parents, and mentees tell me how much our mentoring program meant to them. Some of the relationships between mentor and mentee continued from elementary school into high school. That's amazing! What I have learned is that school needs to be more than a place where students learn academics. It needs to be a place where students feel safe and cared for. When that happens, then the rest comes naturally. Mentoring helps us make school THAT place for kids.

~ Dawn Turner, Principal,
Benson Elementary School, Itasca, Illinois

If reaching out to multiple schools sounds daunting, keep in mind that for you to begin a school-based mentor program, you only need one school. Gaining greater clarity about the issues and questions surrounding the initiation of a school-based mentoring program is essential for gaining acceptance for such a program.

In addition to the materials given to me by the Chippewa Falls program, I also used a resource from the Search Institute in Minneapolis called *40 Developmental Assets*. This research group identified forty building blocks of healthy development for young people. Possessing these assets will help students grow up to be healthy, caring, and responsible citizens. (A link to this site is listed in the resource section in Chapter Six.)

Within these developmental assets, seven of them are particularly apt in supporting the value of school-based mentors and helped me make my case for the benefits of supporting a program. These assets include:

- *Other Adult Relationships*: The young person receives support from three or more nonparent adults
- *Caring School Climate*: The school provides a caring, encouraging environment
- *Community Values Youth*: The young person perceives that adults in the community value youth
- *Adult Role Models*: Parent(s) and other adults model positive, responsible behavior
- *Achievement Motivation*: The young person is motivated to do well in school
- *Bonding to School*: The young person cares about his or her school
- *Sense of Purpose*: The young person reports that "my life has a purpose"

These assets reflect so much of what can come from mentoring. Mentors provide positive support for students, and when they connect with students, they become an additional role model who will be a motivator, a trusted and caring friend, an encourager, and a strong supporter of the student.

The entirety of *40 Developmental Assets* makes a convincing case that effective mentors:

- Provide strong support for students in school-based mentor programs
- Open another avenue of support for students
- Come with an open mind and add to the positive school atmosphere
- Offer another listening ear and provide opportunities for one-on-one conversations without interruptions
- Are there to listen and offer choices of responsible behavior
- Praise and encourage mentees at every appropriate opportunity, providing much-needed positive affirmation

As my conversations with education and community-focused constituents continued, it was time to put together the pieces for our new mentor program. These are important considerations for a larger mentoring effort. We compiled lists of mentor-mentee activities and assembled resource booklets for our mentors. We designed a logo for the program and selected a name. I met with the chief of police and superintendent of schools to determine the type of security checks we needed for mentors. A volunteer created a financial record system for AIMS and also kept contact information for mentors, mentees, administrators, and site coordinators of the various schools, while another volunteer printed our mentor manuals.

Now that we had done the preliminary work in beginning a mentor program, it was time to move on to the important step of recruiting mentors.

RECRUITING MENTORS

To build a sustainable mentor program, you need individuals who are willing to give their time and energy to children and young adults. But how do you go about finding kind and compassionate individuals, and when you do, how do you recruit them?

I knew the recruitment of mentors to sustain AIMS would be a formidable task. We had enough seniors from our JOY group meetings to get the mentor program started, but what if the demand for mentors skyrocketed? For AIMS to meet the needs we identified in our schools and communities in the Roselle area, it required mentors to be recruited for five different school districts representing five local municipalities.

The best way for me to offer guidance about the recruitment of mentors is to share some guidelines I embraced, as well as to share a few of my recruitment stories with you.

Have Consistent Focus

Be regularly mindful of the importance of recruiting new mentors. Bring mentoring into conversations with your friends. At some point, you might say, "You would be a good mentor. Have you thought about being a mentor at a school?" Keep planting seeds for mentors.

Keep a List

A compilation of mentor prospects is helpful. Record the names of those who would be good mentors, along with their contact information, when available. If someone says that they are unavailable to mentor now, but perhaps they could serve later, note this information. If a mentor prospect is uncertain about whether they want to become a mentor, keep their name as well. When attending meetings or social events, be prepared to add names to your list. Keeping a list of prospective mentors is essential for inviting potential mentors to serve with you when additional ones are needed.

For example, for me, this list was helpful when social workers and mentor site coordinators requested a mentor for a student in the middle of the school year. This presented an interesting challenge as I usually did not have a mentor available. When mentors are trained, it is important to connect a new mentor with a mentee as quickly as possible. Recruits who have been trained but who are not assigned a mentee may become easily discouraged. When new needs arise, having this list was essential in matching a potential mentee with a mentor.

Location! Location! Location!

If a mentor program includes more than one school district or community, schedule mentor training classes at local schools and business sites. Prospective mentors feel more comfortable attending a training class at their local school. Providing convenient training locations is advantageous for the recruitment of new mentors.

Get the Word Out

You won't volunteer to be a mentor in a school if you don't know mentoring is taking place in your community. Partner with your local schools to provide solid communication about mentoring opportunities. For example, the teaching staff of Benson Elementary School in Itasca, Illinois, planned a mentor awareness campaign for their community as part of their mentor recruitment strategy. The staff members chose different approaches for sharing the story of school-based mentoring with the community. In addition, a local bank made space available on their outdoor digital sign to announce the next mentor training session date. Mentoring was highlighted in the community school district newsletter as well as the weekly newsletter to parents. An article about the mentor program was published in the local newspaper. The principal of the school and I met with the human resource associate from a corporate headquarters in the community. We shared our story with her about the need for more mentors at the school and eventually recruited seven new mentors from that facility.

Invite Retirees

As people retire, they usually require some time to plan the next phase of their life. They often don't want to load up their schedule right away with new activities. Because mentoring is not a time-consuming activity, only thirty to sixty minutes per week, it is a good time to suggest mentoring to such individuals as a future activity.

Ask Relatives and Friends

Your existing acquaintances may provide a source of mentors. Casually share the mentoring idea with them, taking care to use small pieces of information about mentoring to pique their curiosity. The interest level of your family and friends will dictate your next step. Perhaps you will need to accept their reluctance to be involved in mentoring. They might have questions you can address. Or they may wholeheartedly embrace the opportunity. A discerning and thoughtful response to the level of interest of each individual is important in maintaining both personal relations as well as a good reputation for your fledgling program.

Recruit College Students

If a college or university is located near your school, recruit mentors there. Some colleges and universities require students to serve the community for a designated number of hours. Mentoring is a great way for students to fulfill those hours. College students also like to use these opportunities to build their résumé.

Speak at Civic Group Meetings

Civic groups, such as the Rotary Club, Lions Club, a local Chamber of Commerce, etc., typically have some educational feature at most meetings. Scheduling a sharing time about mentoring opportunities is often possible with these groups. These nonprofit groups typically reach out to the community with helping hands through their volunteer activities, and hearing about the need for mentors provides another opportunity for individual members to consider.

Embrace Varied Vocational Backgrounds of Mentors

Mentors may be recruited from all walks of life. For example, AIMS mentors included two active police chiefs, one mayor, a retired mayor, the president of a bank, more than ten bank employees, a fireman, employees from a corporate headquarters, a real estate agent, the owner of a handyman business, a school superintendent, two school principals, grandmas and grandpas, moms and dads, and retired teachers. These mentors also included AIMS Advisory Board members, a real estate and development company owner, a chiropractor, a social worker, and a resort administrator.

Stories from My Own Recruitment Experiences

My personal recruitment strategy is to talk one-on-one with people I know . . . and with complete strangers! Here are a few stories from my recruitment work:

I saw Kay at the local Fourth of July fireworks celebration at our community high school. She was selling glow sticks as a fundraiser for the local historical society. Kay had just retired as the administrative assistant to the superintendent at the local high school. I walked over to her and congratulated her on her retirement. I also wanted her to know about the AIMS mentoring initiative and inquired whether she might be interested in becoming a mentor. She let me know that she was not going to get involved in any new ventures at that time. I don't give up easily and explained to Kay that just a few more mentors were needed to get the program started. She eventually said she would attend a mentor training session. After she completed the training, she said she would *try* mentoring. She ended up mentoring a single student in a local elementary school for a full year!

This was not the end of the story. We needed a secretary for our Mentor Program Advisory Board. Kay was well-organized because of her administrative experience, so I asked her if she would serve as secretary. She graciously accepted the invitation and served in this capacity for ten years!

———◦∿∿◦———

After leading a mentor training session at a local elementary school, I saw a grandma and grandpa walking home with their grandchildren. I greeted the grandparents and told them I had just finished training mentors at their grandchildren's school. "What do mentors do?" they asked. I explained that mentors spend one lunch period at school interacting with the same student week after week to be a positive role model for a student. The grandfather said he would like to learn more, so he gave me his contact information, and I told him he could expect a call the next day from the principal of the school. He ended up not only mentoring but also volunteering his time helping additional students at the school for many years.

———◦∿∿◦———

I was waiting in a long line at the post office to mail a package. Since I was waiting, I turned around and talked with the person behind me. The gentleman noticed my box was being sent to Japan. I told him my daughter teaches in Japan and that I was also a teacher. He responded that his parents and all his siblings were teachers . . . He was the only one in his family who wasn't. I asked him, "Would you like to be a teacher?" He said he had indeed thought about it.

I told my new mentor prospect about AIMS. After mailing our packages, he followed me to my school to pick up mentor materials and a mentor registration form. He filled out the registration on the spot and attended a scheduled mentor training class the next week.

———⌇⌇———

Notice how all three people were recruited by the same means? They were spoken with directly and invited to consider becoming a mentor. The integrity of the program and the description of the benefits of mentoring for both parties were persuasive and elicited a positive response from the conversations. As I am sure you have noticed, I enjoy the process of recruiting and training mentors. It became my personal challenge to tell my mentoring story to as many people as possible.

However, while I'm more of a "one-on-one guy," enjoying and valuing individual conversations, there are certainly other options in recruiting mentors—particularly in getting the initial word out. You can advertise in your town's newsletter, hang a flyer in your local coffeehouse, make a presentation at a PTA meeting, or put the word out in your church bulletin. Social media, such as Facebook, Instagram, and Twitter, can serve to create interest.

Consider in advance how you would like to be contacted by those interested in mentoring. It would be good to make it as easy as possible for a prospective mentor to communicate their interest to you, so phone calls, e-mail messages, and responses through social media may all be ways for the initial communication to be established. Once a contact has been received, following up with anyone who shows interest is essential in making the kinds of connections that result in securing future mentors.

Training Mentors

Now that you have people interested in becoming mentors, how to properly train them for their role may be considered. The choosing of the trainer is important. A strong mentor trainer is essential for your school-based mentor program to be effective. Usually, one person leads the way in starting the program in a school. It could be the superintendent, a principal, a social worker, a teacher, a person from the community, or . . . you.

With AIMS, I led all the mentor training sessions during the first three years. Not only was I personally invested in this project, but at my stage of life, I also had the time to fulfill these obligations. Later, two other principals volunteered to lead mentor training classes as well. All training sessions were open to any new mentor wishing to serve in any of the schools associated with AIMS.

Selecting a Mentor Trainer

This mentor trainer should have an understanding of the program, a strong passion for mentoring, and should:

- Understand the important role mentors play in supporting students

- Be a person who enjoys telling the mentoring story in a way that motivates the attendees to become mentors
- Be able to communicate the clear role a mentor plays in a school setting
- Be able to tell personal mentor stories so that those in attendance are motivated to say they will become a mentor
- Be prepared to answer trainees' questions with confidence
- Be an encourager
- Have a caring and serving heart

While there may be people with a variety of personalities and aptitudes that may serve as trainers, each trainer should ideally possess, at minimum, the characteristics listed above. Selecting the right mentor trainer is critical, because the mentor training presentation is your chance to make a good first impression on your potential mentors.

Preparation for Mentor Training Sessions

Before a session begins, the trainer should be prepared to respond to questions such as:

- What is my time commitment?
- What is the grade level of my mentee?
- What should I do if I have an unexpected schedule change on the day I mentor?
- If I have questions, with whom do I speak?
- Where will I meet with my mentee?

- Will I be notified if my mentee is absent from school on the day I mentor?
- What happens during a mentor session?
- How can I be sure I am making a difference in the life of my mentee?
- Where do I get my background check?

The goal is to offer the right amount of information. There is a great deal of material to share, but at the same time, you do not want people feeling overwhelmed and doubting whether they have made the right choice.

While presentation software and other digital media tools can be very helpful in engaging your trainees, you can survive without it. What you cannot survive, though, is having a disorganized and uninformed trainer. Make sure that your mentor trainer is ready to get the job done, and put the entire process in the best light for your potential mentors. You want them to feel as comfortable and at ease about the coming steps as possible.

Mentor Training

Training new mentors is a joy! Whether there are two or twenty-two prospective mentors in attendance, one can take pride in knowing they are filling an important role in meeting the needs of children through this training!

Once your mentor trainer is properly prepared for leading an engaging presentation, it's time to begin the training process.

When those mentors-in-training arrive at the session, make sure they are greeted warmly. Thank each of them for attending, and then have them sign a registration form so that you may verify their attendance for future reference. Provide them handout items such as the mentor handbook, an outline of the training session, a mentor application form, and other support materials you may have created. Strive to make them feel both welcomed and excited for the journey they are about to take. If you aren't enthusiastic about their journey, it will be difficult for them to share that enthusiasm!

For my very first AIMS training sessions, I have to admit I did not know what the responses of the participants would be. It turned out to be a gratifying and encouraging experience! While each trainer has the freedom to tailor their approach to their presentation style, I used presentation software to communicate issues that are a part of a typical mentoring process. I also made the session as interactive as possible, creating plenty of opportunities to ask questions. One effective strategy included asking the trainees to think about and share who their mentors have been. The responses were numerous and meaningful. Phrases like "listened to my concerns," "became my good friend," "helped me through some tough times," "was not judgmental," and "laughed a lot," were repeatedly articulated. Talking about the characteristics of a mentor emerged as an inspirational activity. This helped our prospective mentors understand more about the role of a mentor.

I developed a mentor handbook which I used as a foundational resource in those sessions. This handbook was based on many of the ideas shared by the Chippewa Falls program. I then edited this content to fit the unique circumstances of AIMS. (NOTE: A link to the mentoring information from Chippewa Falls is included in Chapter Six.)

Here are several comments that I believe were essential to use in each training session to effectively frame the important aptitudes and role of effective mentors:

- Each child is unique. Mentors are wonderful at discovering the buried treasures within their students. Concentrate on these good qualities and actions, no matter how small.
- Confidentiality is absolutely essential. Mentors quickly become trusted friends of their students, and we do not want to betray that trust.
- In deciding what activities to do at your scheduled mentor meeting time, take your cues from your student. Is he or she upset and just needs to talk? Is she or he ready to work on a project? Would playing a game be best today?
- Remember that relationships develop over time. Patience, persistence, and a sense of humor are valuable assets throughout the mentoring process.
- A mentor is a wise and trusted friend and guide; a mentor is a listener and can be a coach, a cheerleader, a confidant, and an advocate.
- Most of all, enjoy each other as friends!

Since the trainer may only have one opportunity to influence a new mentor prospect, the training presentation must be convincing and provide a clear vision of their responsibilities as a mentor. One of the ways to do this is to embed mentoring stories into the presentation. As previously mentioned, to initiate the conversation, ask those in attendance to talk about their personal role model/mentor when they grew up. Adults are typically quite willing to talk about the people who made a difference in their own lives. Engage participants in a discussion about the characteristics of an effective mentor. The stories shared help mentors in training understand the positive role they can play in the lives of their mentees.

Here are some key topics that need to be covered in the training session:

CONFIDENTIALITY:

This is an essential topic in mentor training. Mentors must protect the confidentiality of the student and must not share stories that are entrusted to them. Trust is fragile and, once broken, is not easily regained. All information mentors learn from their mentees, or is told to them about their mentees, is confidential, and sharing this information is a violation of confidentiality policies. However, if the mentee tells the mentor something life threatening, it must be reported immediately to the school principal or a guidance counselor. Examples of this are child abuse, physical abuse, sexual abuse, general child safety, or self-injury. Typically, every school has established procedures for dealing with these kinds of revelations, and it is critical that school administrative staff is notified if these serious situations are revealed. It is NEVER the role of a mentor to make a judgment about the truth of these allegations or to use them as fodder for gossip. The role of the mentor is simply to report the information properly to school authorities, who will then handle the situation.

PUNCTUALITY:

Mentors must keep their appointed session times. If there is any schedule conflict with the scheduled time to mentor, mentors should be advised to call the school with this information. The student counts on the mentor being there at the specified time. Don't disappoint the mentee without exceptional cause.

BACKGROUND CHECKS:

Mentors are required to have background checks completed, and depending on your district, there may be additional requirements before a mentor may serve within a school building. The school should provide the trainer with the necessary forms to be handed out during the session.

WHAT TO EXPECT:

The most often asked question at mentor training sessions is, "What do I do at my mentoring session?" Simple games are an easy place to start. I have seen mentors and their students playing games like Chutes and Ladders or more difficult games such as chess and cribbage. One mentor brought his coin collection to the mentor session. The student was interested enough to start his own collection with the help of his mentor. One mentee taught computer skills to her mentor.

These are just a few ideas to get mentors started. Emphasize to the trainees that no matter what one decides to plan for their mentee, it is most important to engage the student and seek to enjoy each other's company. Ultimately, it is less about the **doing** and much more about the **being**. The doing can provide the opportunity for the mentor and mentee to connect, but the most important thing to bring to your session is your attention and readiness to listen.

FOR THOSE WHO CANNOT ATTEND A TRAINING SESSION:

Have an alternative plan for those with whom scheduling a training session is difficult. You do not want to lose prospective mentors because they cannot make it to the scheduled training session, so make sure you have some viable substitution to offer them. It can be a video of a training session that you can hand out as a DVD or provide a link to access online. When AIMS first started, we provided a videotape of our mentor training session for the prospective mentor to watch at home. They then met with a site coordinator at a convenient time to review key concepts of mentoring that we shared in the traditional training sessions.

A volunteer coordinator from a school district in Illinois

described the importance of both volunteers and training in this way:

I am of the firm belief that volunteers are an integral part of a good school system. In a time of high expectations for teachers to meet the needs of every child in his or her classroom, most staff should be anxious to have the support of "unpaid staff," as I like to call volunteers. Volunteers clearly enrich students' learning experiences and serve as a wonderful resource for teachers and administrators who are wise enough to utilize this help.

Not only are volunteers in schools great advocates for learning, but they also help to create and maintain a nurturing environment and caring sense of community which all children can benefit from. In the busy world we live in today, with many homes having both parents working, or with single-parent homes on the rise, the amount of time spent at home helping with schoolwork continues to decrease, putting more work back on the teacher. Sometimes, it's the classroom volunteer, be it another parent, grandparent, or a concerned community member, that provides the support that the parent and teacher are not able to provide.

I believe that volunteers in schools empower children to want to achieve their full academic potential; after all, they are there helping the children because they want to be, not because they have to be. Sometimes, it takes a fresh set of eyes and extra helping hands of a volunteer to get through to a student who is struggling. Sometimes, it takes a retired person sharing a valuable life lesson—a transfer of knowledge as I like to call it—to help a child realize that someone other than their teacher cares about their education and reminds them that they are smart, and they are special. Sometimes, it really does "take a village" to raise a child.

I believe that George Bernard Shaw put it best when he said, "I am of the opinion that my life belongs to the community, and as long as I live, it is my privilege to do for it whatever I can. I want to be thoroughly used up when I die, for the harder I work, the more I live . . . Life is no 'brief candle' for me. It is a sort of splendid torch which I have got hold of for a moment, and I want to make it burn as brightly as possible before handing it on to future generations."

~ Eileen Delahanty, Volunteer Coordinator,
School District 158, Huntley, Illinois

TIME TO LAUNCH!

If the school has embraced the program, and you have successfully recruited and trained mentors . . . our new program is ready to launch!

For me, it was amazing that in less than a year from the time of our visit to Chippewa Falls, Wisconsin, AIMS was up and running. The first mentor matches in the AIMS program took place in February of 2003. There were no celebratory events that took place when the first students met their mentors. There was no ribbon cutting or speakers to show that we had started. The mere anticipation of the start of AIMS gave those involved a sense of accomplishment. The number of mentor-mentee matches grew quickly. By 2005, the total count of volunteer mentors grew to sixty-five, with ten volunteers serving on the advisory board.

Why did the launch of AIMS happen so quickly? It was because many dedicated individuals got involved and supported AIMS. Again, though, let me remind you not to feel pressured to create a program as large as AIMS. Remember that it had a ministry firmly behind it right from the start. But do not be surprised if your work touches upon an important school and community need and is embraced very quickly.

LIFT UP MENTORS:

Once your program is up and running, and your mentors are giving of their time and talents, make opportunities to recognize and thank them. This is a great way to remind them that what they are doing matters. Examples of acknowledging and uplifting mentor volunteers include giving gifts such as potted flowers, recognition pins, or notepads to our mentors at the end of the school year. At AIMS, we established a celebration at the local high school that recognized mentors. This recognition also provided a dedicated time for parents and students to interact with the mentors and thank them for their service. The well-attended milestone event became an annual highlight of the mentoring calendar for parents, mentees, and the mentors themselves. Strong support for mentors provides the incentive to continue mentoring year after year.

PREPARE TO SHARE:

It is natural to be intently focused on building a specific program, whether it be for mentoring or for some other purpose. It takes both mental and physical energy to build and lead an organization. One's thoughts may be consumed with details and next steps to the point where it is challenging to think about much else. Therefore, opportunities to share your work with others may be far from the forefront of your mind.

Yet, once an initiative is established and has built a good reputation, it seems as if others will start to take notice and want to know more. That was certainly true with AIMS. In the years after the program opened, I began to field requests for information about what we were doing. These inquiries led to speaking engagements, site visits, the sharing of program resources, and other such activities. As I saw that what we had built with AIMS was of interest to others, I began intentionally to seek out opportunities to share about AIMS and mentoring. Why keep these things to ourselves? So many more students could benefit from mentoring if we were willing to share our story and resources.

In time, AIMS became the model for similar mentor programs in AFC School District 275 in Franklin Grove, Illinois; Redeemer Lutheran School in Springfield, Missouri; Grayslake North High School in Grayslake, Illinois; and St. John's Lutheran School in Lombard, Illinois. The pattern for how these schools and districts came to embrace a school-based mentoring program was similar. Often, I received an initial e-mail requesting information. Since I had the mindset that I wanted to share as much as possible and support mentoring in all forms and places, this initial contact typically led to larger personal conversations about mentoring and program building. While each new inquiry led to its own unique path of communication and implementation, I was often invited to visit these new sites and provide training and support.

The sharing with Grayslake North High School was unique in that AIMS initially had little connection to secondary education. Megan Sayre, a former member of Trinity Lutheran School where AIMS was founded, was a social worker at the school and sought to implement mentoring within her building.

Because organizing a mentoring program at the high school level was new to me, I asked her to share how her program works. The main difference was that mentors were recruited specifically from teachers and staff already employed by the school, not volunteers from the community. Here is an excerpt from her letter:

I am the AIMS Coordinator and receive student referrals from teachers, guidance counselors, parents, and even students. Any student referred is eligible for the program. Teachers and other staff members at the school (secretaries, hall monitors, guidance counselors, and administrators) volunteer to be mentors, and I train them when they enter the program.

All students need signed parental consent forms. I allow mentors to choose the student(s) they mentor based on their previous interactions with the student, if any, and schedule similarities. It is not necessary for the teacher and student to have the same lunch hour, study hall, or to have a class together, but it is certainly helpful. We do not have time built into our schedules for the mentor/ mentee pairs to meet. It is up to them to decide how often, when, and where to meet. Some pairs eat breakfast together at the school cafeteria each Monday before school or have lunch together. Some rarely see each other due to busy schedules but e-mail back and forth. Others send cards. Some students meet after school for homework help. Some students meet with their mentor to talk about personal issues. Some mentees need assistance with class selection and also choosing the right university. Other mentor-mentee matches attend athletic games together or volunteer to work together at school events.

Some mentors feel very connected to the program, and others feel less so. Ultimately, they get out of it what they put into it. The only stipulation is that they must hang out on school property or at school events. So they can see a school play together on a Saturday night if they meet here at the school, but they can't meet at Starbucks for coffee. Three to four times a year, I organize social events at the school for the mentors and mentees to see each other. So far, we have had Fall and Valentine's Day breakfasts, ice-cream socials, and game nights. We currently have fifty-five mentors and seventy-four mentees.

For me, planting seeds for new mentor programs quickly became one of my new goals. This didn't happen until after I had coordinated the AIMS Mentor Program for several years. I was pleased with its growth but still wanted to help others start new mentor programs. My focus, while still with AIMS, was drawn to the needs of other communities as well.

Reading about the experiences of those with whom I shared AIMS has been a joy. One mentor from Springfield, Missouri, took the time to share the following thoughts:

It has been an interesting two years with my mentee. He's very pleasant and fun to be with. We are meeting in the library while he eats his lunch, and we have begun a major Bunco competition. I don't know if you have a chapter on rolling dice with your mentee in your book, but we have fun. The time goes by quickly and is especially helpful if my mentee wins.

I always enjoy being in the halls of the school, trying to absorb some of the boundless energy from the kids, getting hugs from my grandson and granddaughter, plus having many children call me Grandma. My mentee's teacher commented last week that he appreciates my coming in to visit and that my mentee smiles when he sees me.

Mentoring is a wonderful way to connect with a student. Both the mentor and the mentee receive benefits. It's a win-win activity.

~ Katie Schmidt, mentor
Redeemer Lutheran School,
Springfield, Missouri

Obviously, there is no "one size fits all" or cookie-cutter method of building a program. The key is to clearly communicate the core elements of sound mentoring programs and practices to be the roots of a new program and then nurture it to grow the way that works best for the students served within that school or community.

Some of those seeded mentor programs blossomed and grew, while others lasted just a couple of years. Some programs mirrored ours, while others took a different direction. I am grateful to have had the opportunity to plant those seeds in other communities and schools. While not everyone might have the mind-set of sharing in this way, intentional sharing is certainly something to consider if one seeks to multiply their impact through mentoring programs.

In reading this chapter, it might be easy to conclude that school-based mentoring is the only type of mentoring that has value. Not true! Mentoring can take many different forms. Keep turning the pages as other mentoring models are revealed, and perhaps you will discover a role in which you can invest in the life of another person.

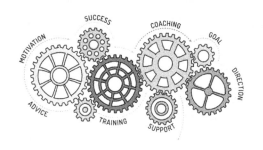

CHAPTER FOUR
OTHER MENTORING MODELS

"It takes a whole village to raise a child."

~ African Proverb

It has been a joy and a privilege for me to share the ways that mentoring has impacted my life, both as a mentor and a mentee. And I am sure it is clear that I am passionate about the value of the school-based mentoring model. Yet, our discussion of mentoring is still incomplete. While school-based mentor programs impact the lives of thousands of children each year, there are many more formal and informal mentoring opportunities to explore.

Are you already a mentor? Perhaps you have never considered the question, but the answer is almost certainly a resounding, "Yes!" You may or may not be fully aware of your mentor status, but the odds are extremely high—especially if you are someone over fifty—that someone, knowingly or unknowingly, sees you as a mentor.

If we intentionally reflect on our lives, each of us has opportunities to support people of all ages through positive comments, caring words and actions, or listening to others and asking thoughtful questions. We all can provide needed support for someone. And we don't need a program like AIMS to meet the needs of others!

We must never underestimate the value of the contacts we have with our existing family and friends. They are priceless. You never know which people have been touched by your kindness and support. God allows each of us to embark on a unique journey in life—one that builds wisdom and perseverance. And that wisdom might be just what another person needs to hear at a formidable moment in their life.

Though the bulk of this book focuses on a more "formal" version of mentoring within a program, it is important to note the significance of other types of mentoring relationships. One very significant relationship is that between a grandparent and their grandchild.

Are you a grandparent? If not, chances are grandparenting is on your horizon. And even if you never have a biological grandchild, you might be asked to serve as an honorary grandparent in someone's heart.

As the father of three children, I phoned my parents three times to let them know they had a new grandchild. I could

tell by their excitement that they had been anxiously await-
ing my call. And why shouldn't there be great excitement?
Most grandparents want to see and hold their grandba-
bies as soon as possible. They have a vested interest in their
grandchildren.

I know I reacted the same way when I received news from
my children that I was a new grandpa. I was thrilled with
the news and thankful for this new blessing. I couldn't wait
to see and hold my new grandchild. I was already thinking
about the types of loving support I could give this new family member.

Grandparents have a special opportunity to be mentors to
their grandchildren. Here are a few examples of unique ways
in which people I know have done this.

AUDREY AND RICK:

Our family friends Audrey and Rick Monson live in the
Denver area. We usually stay with them when we travel to
Denver to visit my son's family. One Monday evening during one of our visits, my wife Karen and I told Audrey and
Rick we wanted to take them out to dinner. Audrey asked
if they could bring their grandchildren Sabrina and Sander
with them and, of course, we said yes.

We learned that Monday is Grandparents' Night in the

Monson family. Each Monday evening, Grandma and Grandpa Monson invite one or two grandchildren to come and have dinner with them. Audrey knows the favorite foods for each of her seven grandchildren and prepares these favorites as often as possible. Who talks with the grandchildren and plays games with them while Audrey is cooking? Rick has this privilege.

When the garden seed catalog comes in December each year, Rick shows the catalog to his grandchildren and asks what he should plant in his garden that spring. One year, they had purple carrots, thanks to one of his grandkids asking for them. Other grandkids wanted watermelon, cucumbers, corn, carrots, and green beans. Rick's garden is a small plot in their backyard, and he can teach his grandchildren about horticulture without it feeling like school. And each and every one of the grandkids loves their one-on-one time with Grandpa and Grandma.

Having a Grandparents' Night is a special time to mentor and build relationships. The seed catalog tradition also is significant in the mentoring relationship Audrey and Rick have with their grandchildren. They will always remember those nights and may even continue this tradition when they have their own grandchildren.

WARREN HIGGINS:

I first met Warren Higgins because my local librarian knew he wrote a book that might be of interest to me. The book is titled *The Wednesday Pen—A Grandfather's Legacy to His*

Family. It is a collection of the letters Warren wrote to his grandchildren every Wednesday for five years. Since Warren's oldest grandchild lives in Montana, this was the way Warren chose to stay in touch with all of his grandchildren wherever they lived. He never missed a week.

The Wednesday Pen provides a grandfather's thoughtful insights on many topics, including business, growing up in the 1920s and 1930s, Higgins family stories, life lessons, the military, politics and government, religion and faith, sports, "things to consider," and other meaningful topics.

Warren's daughter saved all the letters her father had sent to her son Ryan. She published the letters as a way of passing down the Higgins traditions from one generation to another. Warren has a passion for his country, his love of family, and his desire to serve others. He is an encourager, a role model, and an excellent communicator who used his gift of writing as a way to connect with his grandchildren. It also serves as a unique way to mentor—and one that is shared by future generations.

DONNA AND VIDI

Our neighbors Donna and Vidi Morkunas are caring grandparents who intentionally moved closer to their grandsons Kyle and Alec when they retired. They wanted to support their grandsons during those important "growing up" years. Living close by, they could celebrate birthdays and holidays together. Donna and Vidi established a strong relationship with their grandsons during these phases of their lives and were able to see them grow and mature.

During the school year, Donna and Vidi also spent most afternoons at their grandsons' home until their parents came home from work. That time together was special because it helped build strong relationships with them. Their choice to move near their grandchildren was paying the dividends they had hoped for.

Attending athletic events of their grandsons was another priority for Grandma Donna and Grandpa Vidi. The two boys participated in many sports, and that meant traveling many places—and Donna and Vidi were there as much as possible to cheer them on. "A couple of years ago, I missed one of Kyle's baseball games, and he had a great game," Vidi shared. "I will never miss another game." Now if his schedule conflicts with the sports schedules of either of his grandsons, Vidi's first choice is to be there for his grandsons.

One day, I looked out the window and saw Donna and Vidi saying good-bye to Kyle and Alec. It took several minutes to get their grandkids in their mom's car to go home. Donna was talking to her daughter, and Vidi was still playing catch with a grandson. Before they left, Vidi did "a little jig" with his grandson. I could see both of them laughing and having a good time. For me, it was a delight to see a grandpa relating to his grandson in this way.

Grandparents, PLEASE spend time with your grandchildren. Time is short, and soon they will be out of elementary and high school, entering college and choosing a vocation. Don't miss the chance to support your grandchildren at an early age and cheer them on. This is a special task grandparents can fulfill!

———✦✦✦———

Grandparenting: A Ministry of Mentoring, Mattering, Witnessing, and With-nessing

By Rich Bimler,
Ambassador of Health, Hope, and Aging
Lutheran Life Communities

Grandparents have the opportunity, responsibility, and expe-rience to be wonderful mentors to their own grandchildren and the grandchildren of others as well! The Lord continues to provide each of us with so many chances to rub ministry shoulders with children and youth. Look around you—chil-dren are everywhere, waiting to be encouraged and connected.

Here are some handy hints about encouraging each other to mentor younger people around us. To be a **MENTOR** is to consider these techniques:

Mind-set matters! Grandparents certainly need to see them-selves as mentors to their own grandchildren but need not limit their mentoring to them alone. The Lord calls us to minister to people of all ages as well as to people in many different families and communities. Perhaps you are not able to connect directly with your own kin. Accept that fact, and then use your gifts to bond with other youngsters around you. What matters is that we continue to relate with people in helpful and encouraging ways, whatever family they may have joined at birth.

Encouragement matters! There is one thing that all grandparents can do with and for grandchildren: Encourage! Mentoring grandparents encourage grandkids through words, smiles, hugs, gifts, and by their presence. Remember that the three top ways to mentor grandchildren are to encourage, encourage, and encourage!

Knowledge matters! Grandparents have so much information and so many experiences they can share. Their knowledge of history, family, faith, culture, and life itself is crucial for grandkids to hear, learn, and inwardly digest. Yes, grandparents can and should offer their vast knowledge of life to others, as long as we understand that wisdom does not mean we know everything; rather, wisdom means we know that we do NOT know everything! Let us encourage one another to tell our stories of the "good old days," our lives on the farm, and the fact that we walked five miles in the snow each day to school and five miles in the snow back home that same day! Knowledge needs to be shared, our experiences need to be offered, and our feelings need to be expressed.

Teaching matters! Many grandparents who do formal mentoring are indeed teachers of many things: language, art skills, handicrafts, cooking, math, and biblical studies. However, even if we are all not formal mentors, we all are informal mentors as we listen and respond to youngsters' thoughts, questions, worries, and situations. The beauty of a mentoring style of mind-set is that mentoring works for two reasons. Certainly, the youngster being mentored gains from advice and skills, but he or she also has a responsibility of attempting to live up to the expectations and encouragement that the mentor is providing. Teaching matters, both formally and informally.

Opportunities matter! Grandparents are encouraged to seek out opportunities to be mentors, both to their own grandchildren as well as to others. Do not wait for a "Help Wanted" ad for mentors in the local newspapers or a church newsletter. Do not think that people should ask you first. Take opportunities to volunteer. Look for opportunities on your own instead of waiting for opportunities to come to you.

Resurrection matters! What is grandparenting about anyway? Why are we interested in mentoring and mattering to young people? The bottom line is it is all about the Resurrection. We mentor and matter to others because Christ has taken on our lives through His death and Resurrection. Even when we do not do well as Christ's mentees, He continues to mentor us through His love, hope, and forgiveness! We then become mentors to others because we know who matters to us, as well as to all those precious grandkids around us!

⸻

Mainline church denominations have developed processes for mentoring the youth of their congregations. While the guidance and training are spiritual in nature, mentoring for success in other areas of a student's life often emerges. Within the Lutheran church body, to which I have been a lifelong member, this type of training is called Confirmation.

St. Peter Lutheran Church of Gilberts, Illinois, has been my church home since moving to Huntley, Illinois, in 2013. When one joins a new church, one quickly identifies the strengths of a parish as well as the inherent challenges the congregation faces. At St. Peter, Pastor Bruce Milash expressed his concern that religious instruction and the Confirmation process was becoming a milestone to be achieved rather than a lifestyle to be embraced. Far too many young people were not maintaining a connection with their church during high school and beyond.

As Pastor Milash and I conversed about this issue, the idea of intentional mentoring of Confirmation students arose. Perhaps intentional adult mentors who continually connect with his or her mentee during the student's Confirmation instruction, high school and college years, and even beyond, could generate a friendship with caring adults that could last a lifetime. Through a series of conversations that in many ways mirrored the start of AIMS, the congregation chose to embrace intentional mentoring within the Confirmation process.

Providing mentoring in a church setting required many of the steps found in the establishment of AIMS, such as defining the role of a mentor, listing the personal qualities desired for a mentor, setting up background checks, building a training session, and actively recruiting potential mentors. However, there is a difference in the types of activities that support the mentor/mentee relationship. These activities include:

- Greeting mentees when they see them at church
- Sending cards and notes of encouragement on birthdays, special occasions, or simply to show their care and support of their mentee
- Attending plays, concerts, and sporting events of the mentee when possible
- Regularly praying for their student mentee
- Sharing their faith journey with their assigned student
- Helping Confirmation mentees identify opportunities where they can serve others, both in the congregation and the community

If you do provide mentors for students as a part of their religious training, you will involve more people in the shepherding process of serving and caring for young people for the future. Not only will the studenets be blessed, but the mentors will have the opportunity to have another friend for life.

As a former school principal, I saw firsthand the power and benefits of another mentoring model, that of intentional vocational mentoring. Any person entering a new work situation is also entering a unique culture—one with both formal and informal procedures, internal expectations, and more and distinctive processes. For some, entering a new place of work is a daunting experience, and time is needed to become acquainted with the expectations. Others adapt more quickly, but all new employees will benefit from intentional mentoring within this setting.

School principals typically address the needs of a new teacher by appointing an experienced teacher to aid them during the first year (or longer) of their work at a new school. That mentor serves as the point person in answering essential education questions, such as how to unjam the copier, what is the proper procedure for filling out report cards, where is the best place to position oneself while on recess duty, and many other queries that emerge during a day. Mentor teachers may also be an important liaison for those who are new to the community, offering advice about the best places to receive common services, such as for car or home repairs, ideas about the best places to shop, the most economical routes to take between two sites, and other seemingly trivial but vitally important pieces of information.

But this type of intentional mentoring is not only a part of schools. Workers in all vocations may benefit from this intentional mentoring, whether it takes place in an office or on a construction site. And mentoring in the workplace does not even have to have a formal and organized approach. If someone is new to where you work, there are always opportunities to approach this person and offer to help answer any questions they might have. That is mentoring—simply being available to provide support and build relationships!

If you look carefully, you will see mentoring relationships all around you. These relationships are not formalized by programs, nor are they even thought of intentionally as mentoring, but they abound throughout life. Have you seen mentoring in these ways?

- A mother (or father) guiding a daughter (or son) in the basics of cooking
- A father (or mother) sharing with a son (or daughter) the basics of home repair
- A baseball player showing a teammate a new bat grip for their swing
- A student offering to help a classmate better understand a math problem
- Women (or men) sharing best practices for the completion of laundry
- Men (or women) collaborating on best family financial processes

What other mentoring activities should be added to this list? If we are thoughtful and observant, this list grows quickly. Mentoring is all around us! It is a part of our socialization. It is an integral part of learning and growth in our communities. God has created us for community with humans, not just for company and companionship, but also for learning and growth. Opportunities to mentor abound!

Are you already a mentor? I have no doubt that you are! One cannot help but be a mentor in our world today, although, hopefully, you have seen in the previous chapters some ways in which your mentoring influence may be targeted and compounded.

As humans, we are drawn to great storytelling. Stories of mentoring are inspiring, varied, and complex. As we move on to the next chapter, be ready to be captivated by the stories of mentors, mentees, and those that have benefitted indirectly by mentoring relationships. Whether you are certain intentional mentoring is for you or are as yet unsure, keep reading!

CHAPTER FIVE
STORIES FROM MENTORING

"I don't think people need to retire and just sit on the front porch and rock. They've had a lifetime of experience. They can pass that on. There's nothing like inspiring a young person in these areas of curiosity of their own, and a mentor can do that."

~ John Glenn

Our review has thus far studied mentoring as an intentional or organic process by which wisdom and support are transferred. Understanding the mechanics of these series of steps helps establish the value of mentoring and how it can best be carried out for the benefit of others. But what about the individuals involved in mentoring? What are their unique stories? How can we distinctively identify the blessings of mentoring for individual lives? Mentoring is not just a process but a lifestyle embraced by many in our communities, and reviewing individual accounts of the power of mentoring is exhilarating and inspiring. Here are some of those stories of the power of mentoring.

For me, while I have certainly grown and benefitted from the opportunity to mentor others, the mentoring that I received at significant moments of my life has shaped and molded me. I experienced this intensive mentoring in my youth in Arcadia, but my professional life has also been blessed with mentors who have invested in me. Perhaps the most important of those mentors was my longtime colleague in ministry, Rev. Charles Mueller Sr.

CHARLIE, MY MENTOR

Pastor Charles Mueller Sr. has been my mentor since 1978, the year he was installed as pastor of Trinity Lutheran Church in Roselle, Illinois. I didn't know much about Charlie in 1978, and I had no clue about the remarkable journey we were about to travel together. I didn't call Charlie my mentor then, as I don't remember the word mentor being used much at that time. However, as I think about our working relationship, Charlie has been my mentor from the day we met and continues to be a positive influence in my life.

My bonding with Charlie happened quickly and naturally. I was serving as the principal of Trinity Lutheran School, and our offices were next to each other, so we spoke together several times each day. Since I had lived in Roselle for eleven years before Charlie came to Illinois, I could share with him my insights regarding the church and community. My role was to support the new pastor, and I wanted to make the transition to Roselle as smooth as possible for Charlie and his wife, Audrey.

I appreciated the chance to spend quality time with Charlie to discuss church finances, Bible class opportunities, church programs, future needs, and opportunities for new ministries. It didn't take long for Charlie to understand how Trinity functioned. He was anxious to meet the members of Trinity, as well as those in the community, and listen to their stories.

It came as a surprise to me that just before Christmas in 1978, Charlie asked me to consider changing my role at Trinity from being the principal of our school to serving as a pastoral assistant in the church. I gave this change prayerful consideration and accepted the position, not knowing what to expect. I now worked closely with Charlie every day. This was the time when new opportunities to care and serve took an incredible leap for me.

One of the key things a mentor does is encourage—and Charlie is a great encourager. Countless times, he has given me words of wisdom that revive me and give me the energy to finish a project well.

Quite simply, Charlie naturally possesses an encouraging spirit. Whether he is interacting with children, teenagers, or adults, his laugh, his stories, his smile, and his pat on the back all provide encouragement. I rapidly understood the importance of encouragement as I watched Charlie live and work. I know I give more encouragement to people of all ages now than I did when I was a teacher or principal. I was too serious then. I now go out of the way to talk to young-sters and teenagers. Though I didn't know it at the time, hav-ing Charlie as my mentor provided me an example of how a mentor should be with their students. It planted a seed in me that eventually grew into ideas for AIMS.

Charlie also mentored me in leadership. He often said, "None of us is as smart as all of us." Teamwork became a style of leadership for both of us. It takes a skilled leader to build a strong team with common goals and real teamwork, and I gained teamwork skills working with Charlie as my mentor.

I respected Charlie's approach to change. While change is hard for most of us, Charlie helped me understand that change is happening all the time. We must embrace change or be left behind. For example, when the world of computers surfaced, Charlie got a computer and made sure the staff had computers, as well. Then, he insisted we receive training. He foresaw their importance and made sure his staff was ready to evolve with the change.

Another example of teamwork is the story of our cable TV venture. One day in the early 1980s, Charlie told me cable television was coming to our community. He recognized television as a ministry tool and asked me to find out what we needed to produce a weekly TV program. After learning what we needed, we soon obtained the television equipment and began training. We named our weekly program *The Trinity Family Hour*, and it was the first public access televi-sion program on our local cable network. The studio and technical capabilities at Trinity grew through the years. The legacy of this program is that the show is nearing its fortieth anniversary—and is now streamed live on the Internet.

In my wildest dreams, I never saw myself being a part of a television ministry, but Charlie trusted me to provide the leadership. Taking on this television project was a leap of faith for me. It was an honor to be asked by Charlie to lead the way for this new outreach to our church members and the community, and a great example of team effort.

Charlie encouraged staff members to praise in public and give constructive criticism in private. This was a practical application for caring and serving. He practiced what he preached, and I learned this was a great and effective way to work with people.

Our church had a "Why Not?" attitude, and I embraced it through the confidence that Charlie instilled in me. Church members were encouraged to share ideas, and if a member suggested an idea for ministry and others supported the concept, we tried to make it happen. Through Charlie's example, I encouraged their ideas and provided guidance for their ideas to become a reality. This created a vibrant church ready to reach out to the community and the world.

I considered it an honor to have been asked to work with Charlie. He made it possible for me to care and serve in ways I had never imagined. I hope each of you is blessed to have someone like Charlie as your mentor—and that you will be a Charlie-like person and become a mentor for a child or adult and provide similar encouragement and guidance.

Having learned so much and grown through Charlie's encouragement, I knew it was time to embark on a new journey: creating a mentorship program . . . and Charlie was there to support me every step of the way.

Charlie was more than merely a mentor to me. Once AIMS was established, Charlie and Audrey embraced school-based mentoring as well. Here is his story as an AIMS mentor.

WHAT DOES A MENTOR DO?
Charles Mueller Sr.

In one sense, a mentor does very little. In another, he or she does a great deal. To show what this means, let me share a bit about the mentee who was assigned to me ten years ago and with whom I met once a week during the school year. The mentor training session recommended we be prepared to play games, read stories, or talk about community or season events. That's not the way things turned out with me at all. Oh yes, I did some of that at first, but most of all, I went with the flow and was guided by what the mentee thought was important.

The beginning of the mentor/mentee relationship was like starting the conversation on a blind date. How well it goes at first depends on you and your date. When the first "date" with my mentee finally took place, it wasn't that hard at all. Mentor/mentee twosomes were spaced around the library, and we could see what they were doing. No two teams seemed to be doing the same things. Some played games. Some read. Some told stories. Some talked about a school event or activities they and their families were planning for the weekend, or next summer, or for a vacation to come. I saw and heard what was going on around us and, in the process, was reinforced by what I was doing or stimulated to try the approach of other mentors.

Another source of guidance came from conversations with other mentors about their experiences. We always did so without breaking any confidences or making fun of our younger friends. In the end, we realized that getting outside advice when we began was helpful, but it didn't take long before each of the mentor/mentee teams settled down to doing what served their interests and answered their needs. Even that varied over time. Mentees got older . . . so did mentors.

Youngsters were assigned to us but not selected by us, and we received basic information about them. We knew their name, a little about their background, and that it was the mentee and his/her parent's choice that they were participating in the program. We were not given their reason for doing so, and we were not asked to report to anyone at the school about our time together. The mentees took care of any reporting. They freely told their teacher, school counselors, parents, and friends about their experiences. They knew in advance as much about us as we knew about them. Any later insights on the part of either of us developed through our conversations.

The annual "grade" we gave and received came at the end of the school year or the beginning of the next when each of us decided whether we would sign on for the mentee's next school year. Sometimes, one or the other of us was unable to continue for a variety of understandable reasons. Sometimes the mentee's needs of the moment had been met, and they were ready to move on in life, just as only a few young people remain active Boy Scouts or Girl Scouts for life. That's okay.

While never having told my young friend (whom I will call Leo) that I was a Lutheran pastor, we still had some interesting conversations about religion as it surfaced naturally in our exchanges. In matters of religion, as well as anything else in general, when he asked a question, I answered it as best I could, including admitting when I wasn't able to do so. When he brought up something from his personal life that he wanted to discuss, we did so as any two friends might. I was neither his teacher nor his parent. I was his friend. I would ask him questions to help him think or see things in a new light. In some cases, I also helped him find the appropriate person to answer his question or help him frame the query he wanted to make.

In time, I found out from Leo that he had emigrated from Poland when he was about three. Two years before our meeting, he had spoken only Polish. Without openly saying so, he wanted to fit in with his classmates and neighborhood friends as a peer. I could tell that he was a bright and energetic young boy and curious about many things. At first, I brought games, but we seldom played them for long. Leo would take the blocks, dominoes, dice of the game, sometime the game board itself, and try to make something else. The game got in the way of what he wanted to explore. He wanted to ask questions and most often, just talk. I was an adult he came to trust who had experienced many things and been to many places about which he wanted to know. Just as important, I was a fresh audience with whom he could share his memories and stories of Poland.

Leo also wanted to talk about cooking. He was so detailed in his explanations about how to prepare certain dishes that at first, I wondered if his mother was a professional cook. I now wonder if he hadn't learned about cooking from programs on TV that he watched when he was alone.

My wife's mentee, whom I will call Laura, was a different child from Leo. She too liked to talk, but things kicked into high gear only after Laura and Audrey played some games using a tablet of paper. That went so well that one day Audrey brought a little chalkboard on which to draw or play. Chalkboard in hand, Laura showed what she really wanted to do. She wanted to play school with herself as the teacher and my wife as the pupil. Laura was serious about this. Each week, she developed a lesson plan, planned assignments, and gave grades. Included were notes commenting on Audrey's conduct that she was supposed to bring home to me.

This was somewhat confusing at first until Audrey figured that what Laura taught each week was a semblance of what she herself had learned that week. In the context of this "school," she would also surreptitiously bring up things she was experiencing there, such as the difficulty she was having getting along with another student at school or with a sibling at home. It was fascinating to watch her seek support or guidance from her mentor indirectly without asking for it as such. At the end of each session in Laura's "school," she gave the pupil a spontaneous hug—Audrey must have been doing well in class!

After ten years, we have Leo/Laura stories aplenty, plus many more that other mentors have shared with us. These stories are not meant to suggest that mentors need any special gifts to serve. They only mean that mentors need to appreciate young people, be able to sit still and listen to what mentees have to say, and then are willing to talk with their mentees as they are exploring what it means to grow older in what, for all of us, is a constantly changing world. Mentoring helps this happen in a protected environment. Remember: The mentee already has a parent and a teacher and maybe a counselor, all of whom have very clear responsibilities. Mentors are active and caring listeners whom mentees have invited into their lives to be an older and interested friend. You, as a mentor, may be the lifesaver they have never had.

Audrey and I were hesitant about mentoring at first. We were not sure we could do it, given the age difference. There was no reason for us to feel that way. Mentoring is not rocket science. It is a matter of applying to one arena of life the biblical principle of loving our neighbor as ourselves. Some apprehension is natural. Most adults don't have a young friend to whom they are not related and one who is not the child of an adult acquaintance. But a one-to-one, cross-generational re-lationship is what mentoring is all about. It is a modern adult experience that not only benefits those who are younger but those of us who are older, as well. At eighty-five, Audrey and I signed on for yet another year of mentoring. Why? We like doing it. It is our twenty-first-century Fountain of Youth. And it just so happens to be fun, too.

Charlie and Audrey's experiences show what we already know: Every mentoring relationship has its own personality, but there is a commonality in how the mentor can be a posi-tive influence for the mentee by listening and caring.

Next, I want you to meet Joey. He was my first mentee, and my experience with him confirmed to me that the energy I was investing in creating AIMS and helping to foster other programs was priceless. Here's what that experience looked like:

JOEY—MY MENTEE

A single mother moved to the Roselle area and enrolled her three children in Trinity Lutheran School. When speaking to other parents, Joey's mom heard about our school men-tor program. She immediately asked the principal about it. She knew her children needed other adults in their support system and requested a mentor for each of her three children. Her oldest son, Joey, became my mentee.

I mentored Joey from fourth grade through seventh grade, which allowed me to build a strong relationship with him. I could sense when he had a concern on his mind. I learned to understand his feelings and to react in a helpful manner to the pressures he experienced.

My first mentoring session with Joey went well. I met him at the lunch room door after he picked up his hot lunch. We then moved to a quieter yet populated site in the building. I asked Joey some basic questions to get to know him better. What schools have you attended? Do you have any pets? Who are some of your new friends since enrolling in school? He was a little shy, as most students would be when stepping into a new school environment, and I could tell that he was not fully acclimated to it.

I encouraged Joey to select what activities we would do together during our mentoring session. If he wanted to play a board game, he could bring his favorite game from home and teach me how to play it, or we could play any of the games provided by the school. Joey also enjoyed sharing knock-knock jokes with me.

Eventually, my first question to Joey at the start of a session became, "How was your week?" He usually responded with a few stories. It wasn't until he was in sixth grade that we spent most of our mentoring time just talking and not playing games. He told me stories about visiting his grandma, playing video games with friends, or watching sports. I let him talk about any topic he wanted, and he covered a lot of territory!

Because Joey was a sports fan, we often talked about our favorite sports teams: Cubs, Bears, Bulls, Blackhawks, and White Sox. He knew what was going on in the sports scene. We enjoyed talking about individual players and close games. Since Joey played baseball and football, he shared stories about his games and gave me the scores each week.

One day, Joey talked about having to go to the hospital because of a football injury. I knew Joey wanted to be a pro football player, so we talked about the possibility of this happening. He understood how difficult it would be to get drafted by a pro football team, but I encouraged him to work toward his goal.

Our mentoring sessions went by quickly because we both benefited from each session. We had such a good time that our time together didn't seem to last long. I gained insights into Joey's life experiences, and Joey knew he had a new adult friend.

During one of our sessions, Joey wasn't very talkative. I waited for a time when he was ready to talk. He soon opened up and said his family was moving again. Just the word "again" was a key to his feelings. His family had moved from one apartment to another several times. This was difficult for Joey to handle. Every time he moved, he lost his good friends who lived close by. Making new friends in a new community is not the easiest thing to do. New and strong relationships had to be rebuilt. This was a time for active listening on my part. I let Joey pour out his frustrations. I could understand his feelings, so we just talked together for most of our mentoring time about moving. One positive element was that he would be able to stay in the same school. This added stability to his life. Joey always hoped each move would be his last move.

I mentored Joey for four years and watched him grow and mature. He experienced frustrations along the way, as any student does, so we had discussions about conflicts he experienced with some students, as well as getting his homework done on time, and respecting teachers and other adults. My mentoring experience with Joey confirmed for me the importance of school-based mentoring. Talking to each other in the hallway at school brought us closer together. I strove to be a good listener and provided Joey the opportunity to share his thoughts. I respected his feelings and tried to encourage him when times were tough. I hope Joey continues to have other adults in his life who give him encouragement and hope. Joey had a lot to deal with in his growing up years. I am thankful I had the opportunity to be his mentor for four of those years.

In 2011, *The Daily Herald* ran a feature article on the AIMS mentor program. The reporter, Susan Dibble, interviewed Joey's mother. The following is an excerpt:

> *Twelve-year old Joey, who has had Ken Black as a mentor for several years, said the first year he was shy and didn't say much, but he enjoyed playing cards and board games with Mr. Black. He learned he could trust him. "Now I can talk to him," Joey said. "He really helped me with my problems."*

Joey's mom said all three of her younger children are involved in the mentoring program. When her older daughter died several years ago, she said her younger children didn't feel they could talk with her about their grief, but they could tell their mentors! "They adore them [their mentors]," she said. "They really do get a lot out of the program."

Joey is now eighteen years old and a senior in high school. His family lives in Georgia. I recently received an e-mail from Joey's mom, sharing, "Joey is now interested in music. He writes his own music and words for his songs. He wants to continue his education in the music field."

～✺～

It is not only the mentees who benefit from the mentoring process. Adult mentors are blessed by this as well. Here are two testimonials about the personal benefits for the mentor:

Mentoring has been such a rewarding experience for me. It is wonderful being in a positive school setting again after teaching for over thirty years. The principal, staff, and students that I mentor are so grateful for whatever I do to help them in their education. I truly look forward to spending time with them each week. It is wonderful to see the children grow in many ways by eating lunch together, playing games, and doing learning activities. Some have challenging home situations, and I'd like to think that I have given them some love and security. Thank you, Ken Black, for giving me the opportunity to be of service to young children that I feel so strongly about. Anything we can do to foster a child's growth is our job (Mr. Rogers quote). And the mentoring program is so beneficial for students, parents, staff, and mentees!

~ Mary Jane

Mentoring was so heartwarming because you don't know each other at the beginning, but during the school year or years, you have formed this special bond/friendship.

Casually having lunch and talking, then playing games, doing a craft, etc., is such fun for the student and mentor. Then when the student begins to know you and asks to skip recess and stay with you instead, that is very special.

I enjoyed beginning with the younger students in first or second grade and moving up each year with them if they stayed in the same school or district. Seeing them grow and learn fills you with joy as with your own child or grandchild. I got to be with one of my students from second grade through the rest of elementary school and then junior high through their eighth-grade graduation. Very awesome!

~ Paula

Here is a letter from a former mentee to his mentor that highlights the importance of the mentoring experience:

Certain people in my life have had such a profoundly positive effect on me—so much, in fact, that they not only bring a smile to my face every time I see them, but they have helped me to realize better who I am as a person. Mr. Dave Decker has stood out as one of those influences. Through his calm demeanor, genuine interest in others, and powerful faith in God, Mr. Decker has taught me what it means to be a Christian, not just in name, but in identity.

As a student in his seventh-grade confirmation class years ago, Mr. Decker provided me with the realization that believing in God's great work can mean so much more than spending an hour in church on Sunday morning. Instead, being a faithful Christian can be something to live by every day. He helped me understand this by providing us with the tools to constantly relate scripture to our own lives. The Bible was suddenly so much more than a collection of stories that were difficult to decipher for the young mind. They were lessons for us to connect with. We were encouraged to self-reflect in his class, whether we were sharing our experiences as a group, or thinking in our heads about the wonderful comfort God can bring us, through both the good and bad times. This is a habit that he has instilled in me to this day because I know that whenever I need it, I can look to God for comfort.

Even today, I still consider Mr. Decker the most enduring influence on my faith. I also look to him as a wonderful friend who is always willing to listen and remind me that God gives us the strength we need, even when He doesn't answer our prayers in the way we might expect or want Him to. Being able to sit down occasionally with Mr. Decker to discuss our lives over dinner and a beer is one of the greatest simple pleasures in my life. Mr. Decker has helped me learn that God wants us to have those wonderful social opportunities, and that positive, trusting relationships with others are one of His greatest gifts to us. Mr. Decker, along with his wife, Joanne, also go out of their way to keep me connected to the church when many my age tend to drift away, and they encourage me to remain active and faithful, as they help to remind me that I have a purpose in belonging to my congregation.

One of God's greatest gifts to me, when it comes to developing and maintaining a steadfast faith in Him, has been Dave Decker. I am so grateful that I have the faith that I do to this day, and that has been in no small part due to Mr. Decker. The power of true Christian mentorship, especially on a young person, is so clearly made evident by Mr. Decker and others like him who have dedicated themselves to spreading the Good News of the Lord to those around them.

~ Zack Poore

———

These stories, and many more like them that have been shared with me confidentially through the years, consistently reinforce my belief in the power of mentoring. These memories all serve to highlight the sublime impact of humans connecting with other humans in support of one another. Mentoring is clearly a power path for making a difference in a disconnected world.

CHAPTER SIX

MENTORING RESOURCES

"It's very important today for young people to have <u>mentors</u> in their lives. It's a life experience, and that's what the young people lack."

~ Senator John Glenn

There are hundreds of Web sites, books, and articles on the topic of mentoring—a simple Google search yields over 413 million results. Of course, no one is going to sort through millions of results to learn more about mentoring. Even reviewing the first page of Google search results may not lead one to helpful mentoring information and advice. As a result, I have selected some mentoring resources to share with you. I have either read or used these resources and found them to be helpful in better understanding mentoring or the building of an organization for mentoring. While you can still type the word "mentoring" in your search engine and find an incredible number of mentor resources that are available to you, it might be helpful to start with previewed resources that someone has already found of value.

NOTE: Full Web sites and sections of these sites are updated or deleted from time to time. Visit the home page of each recommended site to see what topics are covered and navigate from there.

---

http://educationnorthwest.org/sites/default/files/abcs-of-mentoring.pdf

The ABCs of School-Based Mentoring is a ninety-two-page resource manual PDF document. This edition is helpful for those initiating a mentor program. It provides sample documents, such as a volunteer application, a mentor agreement form, a volunteer interview guide, a teacher/counselor referral form for requesting a mentor, a parent permission sheet, and a mentor profile document.

---

https://cfsd.chipfalls.k12.wi.us/mentor/mentor/mentor-handbook.cfm

The Web site for the Chippewa Area Mentor Program provides many helpful resources for those interested in school-based mentoring. It contains a comprehensive handbook with twenty-seven pages of mentor information located under the *Be a Mentor* tab. I used materials from this handbook when I began the process of organizing the AIMS Mentor Program.

Check out the Facebook pages of the Chippewa Area Mentor Program. With just one viewing, you will understand why this is a successful school-based mentor program. There are testimonials and motivational quotes to review. A monthly schedule of themes and activities provides ideas for connecting with the mentees each season of the year.

---

https://www.facebook.com/TheWednesdayPen/

This is the Facebook page for Warren Higgins, author of *The Wednesday Pen: A Grandfather's Legacy to His Family* (see Chapter Four). Warren provides another way of mentoring grandchildren from a distance. If you are interested in purchasing this volume, the book is available on Amazon.com.

---

www.search-institute.org

For more than fifty years, Search Institute has been a leader and partner for organizations around the world in discovering what children need to be successful in life. Their research, resources, and expertise aid those who serve in the mentoring field. Their identification of forty building blocks of development assist these young people in growing up to be healthy, caring, and be responsible adults. These building blocks deal with the support of the child, empowerment, boundaries and expectations, constructive use of time, commitment to learning, positive values, social competence, and positive identity. Mentoring is one way in which these children are supported through these foundations.

I have used the information from the *40 Developmental Assets* handouts for building support for school-based mentoring (http://page.search-institute.org/40-developmental-assets; reprinted with permission from Search Institute). These handouts come in a pad of fifty tear-off copies. Each handout provides the information in English on one side and Spanish on the other side.

Check out hundreds of resources available from Search Institute. These will help you bring out the best in your work with young people. I have used *The Mentor's Field Guide: Answers You Need to Help Kids Succeed, 150 Ways to Show You Care*, and other resources.

---

http://www.mentorconsultinggroup.com

Dr. Susan Weinberger is a nationally recognized expert on building mentoring programs and relationships. Attending her leadership sessions on mentoring during the early days of AIMS provided me with the affirmation that our program would be a strong one.

These are some of the resources available on her Web site:

Mentoring a Movement: My Personal Journey. This is Dr. Weinberger's account of her journey of promoting the youth mentoring movement. It provides insights into how mentoring gained popularity as a key youth development strategy. This book ignited my passion for school-based mentoring.

There are three guidebooks titled *My Mentor and Me* listed on this Web site. These guidebooks are for mentors working with elementary, middle school, or high school students. The volumes were given to our mentors in AIMS as a resource to use in mentoring sessions.

Guidebook to Mentoring, to which there is also a link through the Web site, is an excellent book to assist one who is initiating a mentor program.

You can even order a mentoring-themed necktie through this site. This colorful tie features artwork designed by mentees with dozens of stars and includes printed words like *friend, leader,* and *encourager.* This tie will prompt much discussion with your friends about mentoring.

www.rebeccasgardenofhope.org

Rebecca's Garden of Hope is a faith-based (Lutheran) group from Orlando, Florida, that has developed strong tutoring and mentor programs in high-risk communities. Through these programs, children can feel safe and are encouraged to build on a foundation of Christ to give them strength as they move through this journey called life.

The following two resources are different from the other links shared in this chapter. These are not specifically mentor resources. Rather, they are references to people and organizations that have in some way aided me on my mentoring journey. I am indebted to these people and organizations for their investment in me through the years.

www.richandcharlieresources.com

Charlie Mueller and Rich Bimler created this Web site to "encourage one another" through words, reflections, laughter, wondering, wandering, connecting . . . and lots more. Both Charlie and Rich have spent most of their lives in ministries of encouragement to professional church workers, lay leaders, families, parents, children, youth, congregations, communities, and movements. With this Web site, they continue to promote, affirm, and celebrate ideas and resources that will benefit you and those around you. Add your name to the Rich and Charlie Resources mailing list and receive their monthly newsletter as well at no cost. This has become a must-read source of encouragement for me.

www.aloaserves.org

ALOA (Adult Lutherans Organized for Action) was founded in 1991 with the mission to equip mature adults to celebrate their life in Christ and serve others. ALOA is committed to supporting senior populations in our communities by encouraging and sponsoring adult ministry through events which foster intellectual, social, and spiritual growth. Their quarterly, eight-page newsletter can be accessed online.

This organization holds special significance for me, since their board asked me to write a Mentor User Guide to be distributed to churches as a resource for ministry. As I started writing for ALOA, I reached the point where I decided to put my mentor story in book form. Therefore, the work of this organization served as the motivation and inspiration for the volume you are now reading.

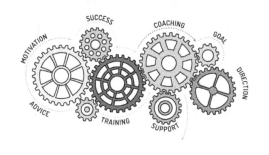

CHAPTER SEVEN

A CALL TO ACTION

"We have different gifts, according to the grace given us. If a man's gift is prophesying, let him use it in proportion to his faith. If it is serving, let him serve; if it is teaching, let him teach; if it is encouraging, let him encourage; if it is contributing to the needs of others, let him give generously; if it is leadership, let him govern diligently; if it is showing mercy, let him do it cheerfully."

~ Romans 12: 6–8 (NIV)

By now, you can probably make a reasonable guess about why I wrote this book. I like telling stories, and I appreciate the opportunity to reminisce about years gone by, remembering the way life used to be. Watching the evening news each day is disillusioning . . . seeing the images of disrupted and disconnected family lives and communities. While there is much happening in our world that is discouraging, I am also heartened by the joy that has come to so many through mentoring experiences, particularly those of the last ten years. There is so much on my heart to talk about and describe.

Through the years, I knew that I had a story to tell. I turned eighty-five years young on May 3rd, 2019, just prior to this book being published. The time to share is now!

But if all I were doing was sharing about my own adventures, this volume would only serve as a personal memoir—perhaps an interesting story about a life of service, but nothing more. And if I concluded this book with just a few more stories, I am not sure my efforts in writing down these life events would be useful. In the end, who am I but one who is simply doing the best I can to serve others—sometimes succeeding, sometimes failing, always struggling. There has to be a much more significant reason for why I spent nearly six years writing this book, and a more compelling reason why you have stuck with me through these seven chapters.

The reason for writing is not for me, but for YOU! Yes, you ARE a mentor. Our schools need YOU! Our communities and churches need YOU! Because an Arcadia community so rarely exists today, our world is craving the guidance and leadership only YOU can provide. Mentoring is more than an interesting activity to help fill the days of retirement. It is an essential endeavor that is needed more than ever for the sake of our children and communities.

Where are you in life's journey? Have you been prepared for meeting the needs of others in ways that were not clear when you were younger? Are you ready to invest more diligently in the lives of others? I hope and pray that this is the case because we need YOU! More importantly, someone out there needs your mentoring more than ever before.

In marketing, this type of plea is known as a call to action. Advertisers want to do more than just tell you about a product. They want you to DO something—to buy! Marketers tell a story for a very specific purpose.

I don't want this to sound crass or opportunistic, but I am not much different from those advertisers. I have enjoyed sharing stories from my life. For someone at my age, the memories of the past hold deep significance and meaning. But these aren't your memories, and the sharing of these life events are only important if they lead to something more—a call to action for greater service.

So, there it is—my call to action for you! Engage! Assist! Mentor! And if you are already doing these things, contemplate how you might be led to make an even greater impact.

How will you answer this call to action? Have you been moved in any way by the mentoring stories shared in this book by parents, school superintendents, teachers, mentors, mentees, and others? Will you review your priorities for the coming years? We all have opportunities, choices, and decisions to make. Each of us has gifts God has given to us to use in caring for and serving others.

How will you use your time—those precious 365 days, 8,760 hours, 52,560 minutes, and 3,153,600 seconds in your next trip around our sun? I would love to answer this question for you, but I can't. *You* are responsible for this answer. As your life changes and you move through the various stages of life, your priorities about how you are using your time may change as well. Is it time for you to become a more intentional and consistent mentor to others? I hope that your answer to this question is a resounding "YES!"

"Me a mentor?" Yes, YOU a mentor! God has gifted you with unique gifts, talents, abilities, and interests—ones which serve to connect and identify with others. You have been placed in a world, nation, and community where your work with others is desperately needed, especially as our families and society become increasingly disconnected. You have the resources necessary (remember Chapter Six?) to discover your own mentoring path. And you have my commitment to do everything I can to support you in your journey.

"Me a mentor?"

ABSOLUTELY!

ACKNOWLEDGMENTS

I wish to thank Dr. John Butts, superintendent of Lake Park High School; Dr. Steven Epperson, superintendent of Roselle Elementary School District 12; and Mr. Reed Sander, principal of Trinity Lutheran School in Roselle for early support of school-based mentoring. Their backing was important to the expansion of the AIMS Mentor Program, which later included fourteen schools.

Because of the solid interest in mentoring from both the public school sector and Trinity Lutheran School, we decided to offer AIMS to all elementary schools as a community effort governed by a community-based AIMS Advisory Board.

It is important also to recognize those who served on the first AIMS Advisory Board. They were: Maureen Bell, president of Harris Bank in Roselle; Kay Cahill, retired executive assistant to the superintendent of Lake Park High School; Cathy Crissey, principal of Spring Hills Elementary School in Roselle; Mark Dwyer, principal of DuJardin Elementary

School in Bloomingdale; Marge Engel, one of the four from Roselle who made the initial trip to Chippewa Falls; Amy Reuter, resource director from Benson Primary School in Itasca; Thomas Roman, police chief of Roselle; Dr. John Butts, superintendent of Lake Park High School in Roselle; and Patrick De Moon, president of the Kara Foundation. I thank these leaders of our community who supported school-based mentoring and served on the board of directors. I am indebted to each of these board members as well as others who served on our board throughout the years, and I am thankful for the unique gifts each individual brought to the board.

Thanks to Steve Board, a retired publisher, for advice and encouragement. Thanks also to the volunteers who helped in the mentor office, including Jane Hove, Beth Weber, and Marlin Schilling. I appreciate your caring and serving attitudes. I am also grateful for those individuals and businesses that provided financial support for AIMS through the years.

Thank you to over 150 AIMS mentors who worked with their mentee once a week at area schools. You made mentoring happen with your compassion and understanding hearts. I am also grateful for all the parents who permitted their children to have a mentor and especially you, the students, who eagerly came to your mentoring sessions. You provided so much joy to the mentors who worked with you.

I received much support from family and friends. My granddaughter, Stephanie, helped with the initial editing of the text. Lisa Ancona Roach, a free-lance writer, assisted with the focus of the book. My son, David, spent his Spring Break helping with the flow of the book. David's wife, Gail, proofread the first round of galley review. Kay Cahill, secretary of the AIMS organization, was an encouraging proofreader. My daughter, Miriam, contributed with a deep and insightful review of the book. Thanks much for all of your help!

To Karen, my wife, I thank you for your help when I had trouble with the computer because I pressed the wrong keys. You have endured my messy desk and office, but I will try to do better in the future. Thanks for your support and love.

I appreciate the support of so many friends who shared their thoughts about mentoring with all of us in this book. These stories and the commitment to mentoring behind them provide hope for the future for our schools and communities.

Finally, I would like to thank my family and friends who were, are, and will always be a very important part of my support system.

WORKS CITED

Dibble, Susan. "A Friend to Students." Chicago, IL: The Daily Herald, 2011. Reprinted with permission of the *Daily Herald.*

Weinberger, Susan. *Mentoring a Movement: My Personal*

Journey. Norwalk, CT: Mentorconsultinggroup.com, 2005. Reprinted with permission.

Search Institute. *40 Developmental Assets.* Minneapolis, MN: 2006 Search Institute. Reprinted with permission.

CPSIA information can be obtained
at www.ICGtesting.com
Printed in the USA
FFHW011439180919
55064734-60758FF